Step-by-Step Strategies for Teaching Expository Writing

by Barbara Mariconda

SCHOLASTIC
PROFESSIONAL BOOKS

New York • Toronto • London • Auckland • Sydney
Mexico City • New Delhi • Hong Kong • Buenos Aires

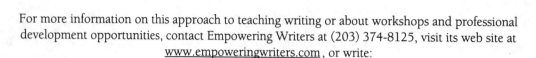

For more information on this approach to teaching writing or about workshops and professional development opportunities, contact Empowering Writers at (203) 374-8125, visit its web site at www.empoweringwriters.com, or write:

Empowering Writers
P.O. Box 4
Easton, CT 06612

If you enjoyed this book, look for these other titles:

The Most Wonderful Writing Lessons Ever
by Barbara Mariconda
ISBN 0-590-87304-0

Super Story Writing Strategies and Activities
by Barbara Mariconda and Dea Paoletta Auray
ISBN 0-439-14008-0

Easy Art Activities That Spark Super Writing
by Barbara Mariconda and Dea Paoletta Auray
ISBN 0-439-16518-0

Front cover design by Ken Powell
Interior design by Sydney Wright
Front cover photograph by Michael C. York
Interior photographs by Glenn Mariconda

ISBN 0-439-26081-7
Printed in USA

Dedication

To Dea Paoletta Auray—a true friend and a good writer

Acknowledgments

Many thanks to all who contributed to the writing of this book:

♦ *Especially to Dea Paoletta Auray for her insight, talent, expertise, creativity, sense of humor, friendship, and her willingness to share.*

♦ *To Linda Chandler and her fifth graders.*

♦ *To all of the Empowering Writers staff, especially Linda Chandler, Kim Hastings, Ruth Lundy, Barbara Morra, and Marion Morra.*

♦ *To Nick and Glenn Mariconda.*

♦ *To Linda Hartzer and Donna Coble.*

♦ *To Wendy Murray, Sarah Longhi, Ray Coutu, and all of the editorial staff at Scholastic.*

Contents

Introduction

Just last winter, after fifteen years as a writer, I experienced the biggest writing challenge of my career. My daughter Marissa, a high-school senior, was applying to art school and struggling with her application essays. She wanted some help. Well, that's what she claimed anyway. I was happy to offer suggestions—and only suggestions—since I felt strongly that the ideas and the writing had to be her own. She agreed, but couldn't get started. Anything I offered was quickly dismissed, despite the fact that she continued to struggle. And moan. And whine. And continue to needle me for advice she would not accept.

My daughter is a gifted artist. Her portfolio was excellent, with a wide range of work in various media, from technically excellent pencil drawings, to well executed oil paintings, to abstract collages. (I'm being strictly objective here, of course—none of what I'm saying is based on maternal pride.) This was fortunate for Marissa, because she was not highly motivated academically, choosing instead to put all her energy into her artwork. I believed she would get into art school on the basis of her portfolio. I also believed that the application essay would be a marvelous opportunity for her to distinguish herself in light of her average high-school record. And the essay had to be good because, in another highly characteristic move, she insisted on applying to only one school.

"Are you going to help me with this or not?" she asked, looking from the application to me and back again. She tapped her fingers on the table and jiggled her foot impatiently. "I just want to get this over with," she added.

I counted to ten and tried to ignore the table vibration.

"The first question," she said, "'Why do you do creative work?'" Then she looked at me, rolled her eyes, shook her head, and sighed.

"Well, why do you?" I asked.

"Because I *like* it!"

I started to lose it before we'd even begun. "Do you actually want to write that down?" I asked. She rolled her eyes a second time.

"Okay," she said, "I do it 'cause I can, like, express myself that way. I get ideas and then I get to see them in the art, you know? It's like, me. It's like I get an idea and run with it and I see where it goes. My pictures are me, when I look at them. They are."

She paused.

I remained silent.

She continued. "That's what I want to say. But I can't, like, just say that. It doesn't sound, you know, smart enough or something."

I tried to help her reword it. We jotted down notes and eventually came up with something that was far more satisfying to me than it was to her.

"I would never talk like that!" Marissa said with a sigh.

"Well, you could always go with your first response," I snapped, "which was, as I recall, 'because I like it!'"

"No," she said, avoiding eye contact.

She struggled on from there, grappling over each idea, each turn of phrase, until she got to something that rang true for her, in a somewhat authentic voice.

That incident was significant to me not only as a writer, but as a teacher of writing as well. Despite years of schooling, my daughter never grew comfortable with expository writing. She struggled to organize an essay properly, even though she could organize her thoughts logically. What troubled me more was that she had such limited experience with the language of exposition that anything I suggested felt foreign to her. Her desire to express herself with truth and honesty made sophisticated word choices and transitional phrases feel false. She had little sense of the ways to address different audiences. She knew it was not appropriate to address a college admissions officer the same way she'd address her peers, but she didn't have the writing skills to make the adjustment.

Now for the good news: Marissa got into her first and only choice, the School of the Museum of Fine Arts in Boston, and is thriving there. Prodding her through those application essays reinforced what I already knew about teaching expository writing—that, as educators, we owe it to our students to familiarize them with the genre's organization, language, voice, and overall construction. If my daughter had had consistent instruction and practice in all of these skills from elementary school on, she would have felt more comfortable addressing the admissions officer effectively in a way that felt authentic to her.

What Do Students Need to Know?

What could have helped Marissa, and other students like her, learn to write more capably and confidently? For students to produce effective pieces of expository writing, they need to know how to:

- recognize well-crafted expository texts
- conceptualize broad, yet distinct, main ideas
- construct broad, yet distinct, main-idea sentences
- ask questions that generate powerful supporting details
- use quotations, statistics, relevant facts, descriptive segments, and anecdotes
- write introductions with attention-grabbing leads and clear, concise thesis statements
- write effective conclusion paragraphs that creatively restate their main ideas
- recognize and develop voice, tone, and slant

My objective in writing this book is to present, in a logical fashion, guidelines for teaching all these skills. I include definitions of them, student and published examples that illustrate these skills in action, and step-by-step strategies for making them clear and understandable to all students.

The Problem With My Writing Program

The book evolved from challenges I was facing in my own classroom. In the past, during writers' workshop, I had my students keep lists of possible topics for process writing. As they worked, I conducted individual and small-group conferences, teaching skills on an as-needed basis.

Although this approach works for many teachers, and I believe in its basic principles, I struggled with it. First, I could never reach all my students. It seemed that out of 23 kids, about 22 needed a conference at the same time—and the one who thought he didn't need one actually did but was bent on avoiding it. Also, no matter how much discussion we devoted to the importance of peer conferences and independent work, I found my students sometimes off-task, talking among themselves and accomplishing less than what I'd anticipated. The students who weren't chatting were usually struggling to get started, while their neighbors were rushing through drafts and were "done" in five minutes. I was often taking time away from conferences to redirect the rest of the class back to writing. In the end, it often took me weeks to reach each student individually. I don't know about your students, but even with peer conferences, writing checklists, and guidelines for working independently, many of mine did not use workshop time well. Often, by the time we met one on one, many were tired of their topics and unenthusiastic about putting what they'd learned from the conference into action and revising. Honestly, I couldn't blame them. The whole process sometimes felt clumsy and frustrating to me, as well. So I changed the way I delivered writing instruction in my classroom.

How I Solved It

As a published author with more than 15 books to my credit, I knew that professional writers approached the craft of writing quite differently from the way most teachers did. I have a large library of books for writers on craft, and I was impressed by the difference between those books and books on teaching writing. All of the books on craft talk about specific skills that can be practiced in isolation. They also talk about the patterns of the various genres of writing.

For example, John Gardner, in his classic book *The Art of Fiction: Notes on the Craft for Young Writers*, says "Fiction is made of structural units; it is not one great rush. Every story is built of a number of such units: a passage of description, a passage of dialogue, an action, another passage of description, more dialogue, and so forth. The good writer treats each unit individually, developing them one by one." While Gardner is referring to narrative writing, the same is true for exposition. William Zinsser, in his classic guide to writing nonfiction, *On Writing Well*, says, "Thinking clearly is a conscious act that writers must force on themselves, as if they were working on any other project that requires logic: making a shopping list or doing an algebra problem."

So I decided to apply everything I'd learned about the craft of writing for writers to my teaching. This meant that my approach would have to change. I began by making a list of what was missing in my writing classroom.

♦ Consistency and assured experiences for all my students

♦ Chances to analyze good expository writing

♦ Opportunities to model the writing/thinking process for my students

♦ Guided practice for students to "rehearse" particular skills without having to tackle an entire piece of writing

In order to fill these gaps, I decided to try delivering all the essential expository writing skills through whole-class instruction. I prepared at least two 40 to 45 minute lessons each week for the introduction and/or review of these topics: writing an introduction paragraph with an attention-grabbing lead and clear thesis statement; conceptualizing and writing broad, yet distinct, main idea sentences; generating powerful supporting details, using quotes, statistics, facts, descriptive segments, and anecdotes; and writing effective conclusion paragraphs in which each main idea is creatively restated.

Each of these lessons was structured to lead students toward independence. Specifically, I would:

♦ **Define and Introduce Each Skill** for the class, using published examples.

♦ **Model Each Skill,** thinking out loud the ideas and questions that might occur to a writer as he or she works. (I took my cue from Zinsser again, who says, "Writing is learned by imitation.")

♦ **Provide Guided Practice.** After modeling a particular skill, I would give my students an opportunity to practice the skill in isolation.

♦ **Encourage Application.** After many modeling and practicing opportunities, students would begin to apply the skill on their own, in timed writing assessments and in their personal writing.

All the lessons in the book follow that sequence. I have included samples of student writing, scripted conversations and actual lessons with students, guided practice activities, and strategies for expository writing and assessment.

Each chapter targets a specific expository-writing skill. You can move through them in sequence or select lessons based on your students' specific needs. Regardless of how you use the book, you will get a good sense of direction, realistic objectives, and step-by-step strategies. Once your students are familiar with a skill, you can look for evidence of it in their writing, after allowing plenty of time for them to practice. You can also assess students' progress using the assessment activities in the book.

I predict that you will find this approach to be sensible, practical, and achievable in the real world of your classroom. And, hopefully, what happened in my classroom will also happen in yours—you will become empowered as a skillful, effective teacher of expository writing. In turn, your students will become empowered as effective, skillful expository writers. And their parents will thank you someday when *they* have the pleasure of watching their children write their college admission essay with confidence, clarity, and individual voice.

𝒲hat Is Expository Writing?

The Reading/Writing Connection

A five-year-old goes off to school for the first time, lunchbox in hand, ready to face the challenges of kindergarten and beyond. There is a lot to learn: getting along with others, sharing, speaking up for yourself, managing time and materials, gaining basic math skills. But, without a doubt, during a child's early years in school the majority of time and energy is spent on learning to read.

This is, of course, critical because once children move into the middle grades, the focus shifts. They must be able to apply reading skills to obtain critical information. And expository texts—texts written for the purpose of informing others—play a big role. Take textbooks, for example. Ideally, middle-grade students learn to skim them for key words and phrases, scan what they have already read, and begin to understand the organization of the text to locate information quickly.

Students need to learn not only how to read expository texts, but also how to write them. In fact, the expository reading strategies students learn (for example, picking out main-idea sentences that identify what entire paragraphs are about) translate into prewriting skills. Understanding the organization of a piece of expository writing is the students' first step toward understanding how they themselves can organize one.

Being able to research, analyze, structure, and present information in writing is a life skill necessary for success in secondary school (remember filling out those blue exam booklets?), college (burning the midnight oil for a research paper), and the workplace (completing the report that was due yesterday). Without a doubt, strong expository writing skills are essential in our information-based society.

In fact, most of the writing we do as adults is expository. Taking notes, jotting phone messages, composing business letters—these are all ways we convey information in writing. These are practical, real-world skills we use in a variety of situations. In this book, I will focus on what is sometimes referred to as "subject writing"—reports, essays, profiles of people, descriptions of places, and recollections of significant or historical events—because that's the kind of writing we expect most frequently from our students. Subject writing requires using prior knowledge, as well as information gleaned from classroom study and/or independent research.

Laying the Foundation for Expository Writing in the Primary Grades

Some teachers begin teaching students the differences between narrative and expository writing as early as kindergarten. As a natural extension of the read-aloud, they pair narrative and expository books on similar topics and compare them using simple summarizing frameworks, such as this one.

Lesson:

Teach the Differences Between Narrative and Expository Texts

My second graders, like so many others, enjoy Arnold Lobel's *Frog and Toad* collections. These stories are narratives, written primarily for entertainment, but they serve as excellent jumping-off points, so to speak, for discussing expository writing.

1. To begin, I gather my students around me in the library corner and hold up *Frog and Toad Together* (HarperCollins, 1972). "Take a look at this cover," I say. The children stare at the drawing of Frog and Toad dressed in dapper pants and jackets and pedaling a bicycle built for two. They giggle at the absurdity of amphibians as fashionable cyclists.

2. I ask students a few simple questions to engage them further:

> ◆ Who are the main characters in this story? (typical response: "Frog and Toad")
>
> ◆ Do you think this story is real or make believe? (typical response: "Make believe")
>
> ◆ Do you think the author wrote this story to entertain you or to give you information? (typical response: "To entertain you")
>
> ◆ How do you know? (typical response: "Frogs and toads don't really ride bikes!" followed by giggles again.)

3. I read aloud a story from the collection, "Dragons and Giants." Then, on a chart, I have the children help me fill in the summarizing framework to the right.

We all agree that, indeed, the story was written to entertain us. It was not written to give us a lot of information about amphibians or bravery or bicycling.

4. I show the children the book *The Fascinating World of Frogs and Toads* (Barron's, 1993). This time, they study the cover photograph of a bumpy brown toad and a slick green frog. The title is printed in large block letters. Once again I question them:

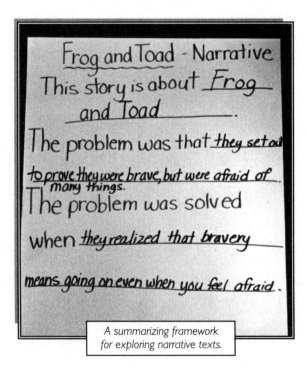

Frog and Toad - Narrative
This story is about *Frog and Toad*.
The problem was that *they set out to prove they were brave, but were afraid of many things.*
The problem was solved when *they realized that bravery means going on even when you feel afraid.*

A summarizing framework for exploring narrative texts.

- ◆ What is this book about? (typical response: "Frogs and toads")

- ◆ So, you mean it's just like the other book? I hold up Lobel's *Frog and Toad Together*. (typical response: "This book is *real!* It's not make believe. It's about real frogs and toads.")

- ◆ What was the author's purpose? Why did the author write this book? (typical response: "To teach you real stuff about frogs and toads.")

5. I read aloud excerpts from *Frogs and Toads*, pointing out text features such as headings and subtitles which help me sort the information as I read. When I'm done, the students help me fill in the summarizing framework to the right.

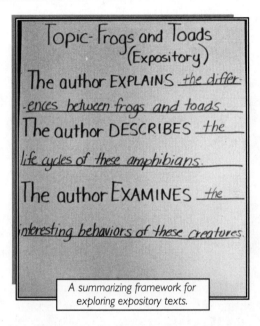

A summarizing framework for exploring expository texts.

Notice that the expository summarizing framework highlights the topic (i.e. what the piece is all about), as well as important main ideas (i.e. differences in life cycles and behavior between frogs and toads). I also use verbs such as "explains," "describes," and "examines" in discussions. This introduces children to the language of expository writing. Throughout the year, I use these summarizing frameworks to draw narrative/expository comparisons between books on similar topics.

Try Reading Aloud These "Side-by-Side" Books

Here are just a few "side-by-side" books that illustrate for young children the differences in purpose, style, and organization of narrative and expository texts:

Expository Writing Author's Purpose: to inform	**Narrative Writing** Author's Purpose: to entertain
Eyes on Nature: Spiders, Resnick (Kidsbooks, Inc. 1995)	*Miss Spider's Tea Party*, Kirk, Neeley, White (Scholastic, 1994)
Hawks, Owls, and Other Birds of Prey, Fourie (Silver Burdett Press, 1995)	*Owl Moon*, Yolen (Putnam, 1987)
Beacons of Light: Lighthouses, Gibbons (William Morrow & Co., 1992)	*Keep the Lights Burning, Abbie*, Roop and Hanson (Lerner, 1997)
The Egg, de Bourgoing (Scholastic, 1992)	*Eggbert and the Slightly Cracked Egg*, Ross (Putnam, 1997)

Building on Knowledge in the Middle Grades

As children move from the primary to the middle grades, a much more in-depth analysis of expository writing is necessary. Students must begin not only to identify the topic and several key main ideas, but also to recognize the organizational plan or framework of a piece of expository writing. This is easier said than done, given the nature, style, and complexity of expository/nonfiction books for older students. My quest for the perfect model illustrates that point.

Choose Nonfiction Books Carefully

I was planning an expository writing lesson for a class of fourth graders. Knowing the value of using literature to teach writing, I set off to gather some nonfiction books to share with students so that, together, we could read, discuss, and point out the characteristics of effective expository writing.

I pulled a variety of books from the library shelves on topics related to our curriculum—the seashore, the saltmarsh, the estuary. Convinced that I had enough useful material, I lugged the whole pile back to the classroom. The kids were in art, so, to my delight, I had 20 minutes left before their return. I opened the first book, drawn to its attractive cover photo of a saltmarsh teeming with life.

Inside, after the table of contents, was a most stimulating, eye-catching spread, containing a huge diagram of the marsh, with birds, plants, and animals labeled. There was a sidebar with a bulleted list of shore birds. Numerous boxes, each devoted to some particular aspect of the marshland, competed for my attention—statistics about our shrinking wetlands, illustrations of the eggs of various shore birds, a map of the East Coast with wetland areas highlighted. All in all, it was a feast for the eyes.

But, as I continued to flip through the book, I found only isolated paragraphs of text scattered here and there, connecting graphics. Clearly, the author's way of communicating information was not with a series of well-constructed, logically sequenced paragraphs. These glossy, illustrated, graphed, charted, side-barred, text-boxed, photograph-heavy books are not always the best resources to use as examples of well-constructed expository writing. They require students to wade through busy pages and reconstruct information in a way that makes sense.

Don't Overlook Magazines

I lugged the books back to the library, plopped them on the counter, and rested for a moment against the bookshelf. My eyes wandered around the room and settled on the magazine shelf, where publications such as *Cat Fancy, Pet Life, Ranger Rick, Sports Illustrated for Kids,* and *Muse* were kept. And, from the looks of them, they had been well read.

I picked up *Appleseeds* (A Cobblestone Publication) and thumbed through it. The issue's theme was "Growing Up in the American Revolution." An article entitled "Sand, Sugar, Sun, Salt, and Smoke" piqued my curiosity and I began to read: "No refrigerators, no freezers, no canned food. How did the colonists keep their food from spoiling? The answer is sand, sugar, sun, salt, and smoke." I was hooked, so I read on. The piece was well constructed, with tight organization and vivid words that delivered a lot of information in minimum space. In other words, the writing, rather than impressive graphics, held my attention, offering information in a most interesting and effective way.

Magazine articles often provide the best examples of tight expository writing for middle-grade students. Once I made that discovery, I subscribed to *Appleseeds*, *Muse* (a Smithsonian Publication), and *Pet Life*, supplementing them with others I often checked out of the school library. This ensured that magazines would be available to students at all times. We began to read the articles together strategically, keeping the author's purpose, structure, and content in mind. One of the ways we did that was summarization.

Summarize a Piece of Expository Writing

Summarizing means reducing a piece to its most essential, critical, key points—in a sense, taking it back to the author's prewriting plan.

I model the process of summarizing by focusing on a topic and locating and restating each paragraph's main idea, using informative verbs. The chart below shows the informative verbs I keep handy for this purpose:

Informative Verbs

outlines	summarizes	informs	evaluates
reviews	studies	examines	lists
assesses	determines	diagnoses	estimates
probes	surveys	understands	unravels
deduces	concludes	draws	gathers
gleans	infers	interprets	tells
surmises	clarifies	defines	details
explains	expresses	spells out	shows
reveals	divulges	devises	fills in
updates	discloses	uncovers	displays
exhibits	unveils	indicates	imparts
describes	reports	recounts	states
analyzes	relates	retells	recalls
shares	reasons	observes	investigates

My sample summarizing frameworks focusing on endangered tigers might read:

> The TOPIC of this book is endangered tigers.
> The author DISCUSSES the traits of these beautiful cats.
> The author INVESTIGATES the ways in which tiger habitat has shrunk.
> The author CONCLUDES that we must protect the tiger to prevent its extinction.

> The TOPIC of this book is endangered tigers.
> The author EXAMINES the traits of these beautiful cats.
> The author DISCLOSES the ways in which tiger habitat has shrunk.
> The author SURMISES that we must protect the tiger to prevent its extinction.

> The TOPIC of this book is endangered tigers.
> The author REVEALS the traits of these beautiful cats.
> The author LISTS the ways in which tiger habitat has shrunk.
> The author ADVISES that we must protect the tiger to prevent its extinction.

I have my students summarize the articles we read using informative verbs and the summarizing framework below. It's amazing to watch how students' vocabularies expand by referring to the chart. From there, students choose different topics and informative verbs and create their own summarizing frameworks.

Initially, I do this kind of critical strategic reading and summarizing in a teacher-directed way. I refer back to key paragraphs within the piece (to highlight the main ideas) by asking students leading questions such as:

♦ What is the author talking about in this paragraph?

♦ What is this paragraph all about?

♦ What is important to remember here?

As students answer, I direct their attention to the chart of informative verbs and, with their input, begin to construct the summary. The summary may have as few as three main ideas or as many as eight, depending on the scope of the piece.

In time, students read with this summarizing process in mind. They begin to summarize independently. Providing a blank framework is a good interim step between directing them through the summary and expecting them to summarize entirely in their minds. Here's what I provide:

The TOPIC of this book is _____ .
The author EXPLAINS _____ .
The author REPORTS _____ .
The author SHOWS _____ .

Each time I present them with this framework I change the verbs, giving them a range of appropriate vocabulary. Eventually they can do this on their own.

From Critical Reading to Expository Writing

These kinds of lessons on reading/writing connections are necessary first steps toward recognizing the characteristics of expository writing. When I first began my new method of teaching expository writing, I felt that, after three or four weeks of initial lessons, my fourth graders would be ready to try their hand at constructing expository pieces of their own. All the expository reading they have been doing would translate smoothly into their own writing. Or so I thought. As the following example from my early attempts illustrates, I had more to learn about how to teach expository writing.

The Kitten Piece

I chose a topic that did not require research and that my students had personal experience with: a pet, either their own or a friend's or family member's. I began by having each student create a web about his or her chosen pet. Here is an example:

Like many of her peers, this student appeared to have a good amount of information to share about kittens. I praised her thoroughness, but I reminded her that I was also looking for specific details— details that would indicate exactly what makes a kitten so cute, the types of toys kittens like, the kinds of games they play, and so on. I also stressed the importance of beginning with an introduction to tell the reader what the piece will be about and ending with a conclusion that sums it up.

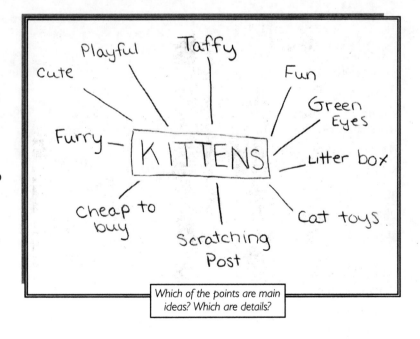

Which of the points are main ideas? Which are details?

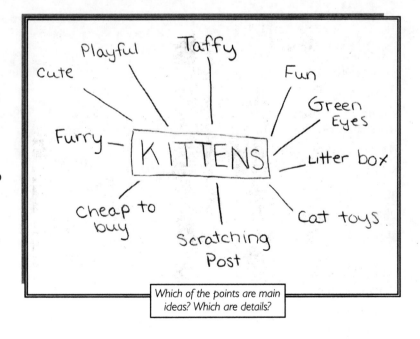

The student nodded and began to write. I felt confident that all of the expository reading, summarizing, and webbing we had done would help her produce good results. Here is the piece she created:

Kittens

    I am going to tell you all the reasons that kittens make the best pets. They are really playful when they chase a ball of string. They are really cute too. They don't need to be walked like a dog does. They are small and furry and come in many different colors. It is easy to get a kitten cause they don't cost a lot.

    You'll need a litter box so they don't make a mess (if you know what I mean). My Grandma's kitten is named Taffy because she is a brownish taffy color. I would pick a kitten with green eyes. I would buy my kitten a stuffed mouse, some catnip, and many more fun toys.

    A scratching post is important so that your kitten won't ruin the furniture. You can find an ad in the paper for free kittens or even a sign on a telephone pole right near your house. They pretend to stalk things like your foot, and then they pounce. Kittens need shots from the vet so they won't get sick.

    So, that is why I would pick a kitten for a pet.   THE END

After reading this student's piece, I shook my head, disappointed—but not totally discouraged. The fact that the student indented at all told me that she had some awareness of the importance of structure. She had a good grasp of the topic, as proven by the variety of supporting details. She attempted an introduction and conclusion. And finally, and perhaps most important, her purpose was clear: She wanted to impart information.

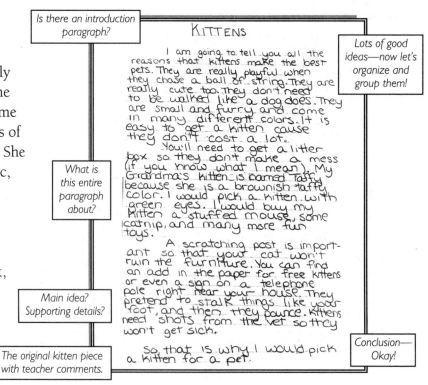

Is there an introduction paragraph?

Lots of good ideas—now let's organize and group them!

What is this entire paragraph about?

Main idea? Supporting details?

Conclusion—Okay!

The original kitten piece with teacher comments.

But as much as I wanted to focus on the good news about the writing, it was clear that the student had not grasped some important principles about expository writing. Basically, she created what I call a stream-of-consciousness piece. She reported anything and everything she knew about kittens. Although she used indents, she used them randomly, without much regard for paragraph content. My hunch is that she knew that longer pieces need paragraphs, and so she indented whenever she'd finished several sentences. She skipped from details about the kitten's appearance to details about its care, from its cost to its playfulness. There were no broad main idea sentences to help readers identify what each paragraph was about. And, while the piece read fairly smoothly, the word and sentence variety were limited.

What the Kitten Piece Taught Me: The Importance of Planning

I learned a hard lesson from this assignment: Even a great deal of teacher-guided reading, summarizing, and webbing of expository text is not enough to create successful expository writers. The jump between appreciating good expository writing and producing it is a really big one!

So the questions for me became: What else can I do to help my students apply their understanding of expository writing to their own writing? What kind of framework do they need to bridge this gap between understanding and creating? What will help them to organize their thoughts logically?

Students need a clear, concise plan in order to communicate information in a way that can be easily conveyed to others. In the next chapter, we'll explore ways to help students discover and apply a plan—a blueprint for constructing an effective expository piece of writing.

Chapter 2

Understanding How an Expository Piece Is Organized

Have you ever had the pleasure (or nightmare, depending on your point of view) of a kitchen renovation? I am living through a massive one now, my writing often interrupted by hammering, a fine white layer of sheet rock dust settling on my computer screen and everything else in the house.

Despite the mess and the inconvenience of life without cabinets, the contractor is efficiently bringing order to the chaos, and the room is starting to take shape. Walls are framed and sheetrock hung, cabinet bases are installed, holes are cut for light fixtures and appliances, flooring is laid. The final details will soon follow—paint, hardware, window treatments—all of the fine points that set your own stamp on the room.

A good contractor makes all this look easy. But what really makes for a functional, beautiful kitchen is a good design. Any contractor worth his or her salt begins a project with a well-thought-out plan. Not even the most talented one walks onto the job and designs the kitchen as he or she goes.

The nonfiction writer and the contractor share a lot in this regard. Both produce better results and avoid lots of painful fix-up work later when they begin construction with a careful, tightly drawn plan.

The Limitations of a Web

For many years, I used webbing as a prewriting framework for expository writing, recognizing its limitations. Remember the kitten piece in the last chapter? I decided to take another look at the web upon which the student based her piece, with hopes that I would gain insights into the way she conceived and constructed it—and some clues as to what went wrong.

While this web was helpful in brainstorming, it did not assist the writer in arranging ideas in a logical, sequential fashion. It did not help her to distinguish between main ideas and supporting details, or to connect ideas to an introduction or a conclusion.

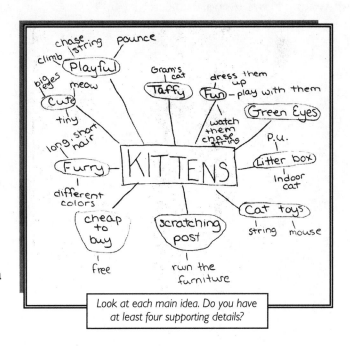

Look at each main idea. Do you have at least four supporting details?

Despite that, I spent years trying to strengthen students' prewriting strategies using a number of variations on this web. I'd list an introduction at the top of the page and a conclusion at the bottom. I'd encouraged students to number each idea in the order they wished to express it. I'd have them list broad details and, to each one, attach more specific ones, like the web to the right.

But even with these richer, categorized details spelled out, the web was not helping my students translate the information into effective expository writing. There was too much overlap. (Notice how "Playful," "Fun," and "Toys" all share the detail about "string"). Some of the broad ideas wound up with no details to back them up. (Perhaps "Green Eyes" should support "Cute" rather than standing alone.)

Now consider my kitchen-design analogy in light of all this. Imagine if the contractor was working exclusively from a web? Can you see him walking in with a sheet of paper with "Barb's Kitchen" scrawled in the center, and all of my dream specifications branching off in random order: "hardwood floors," "wainscoting," "recessed lighting," "almond-hued wood cabinets," "center island with cook-top," "butcher-block countertops," "one glass-front cabinet," and "pantry roll-outs." How successful would he be installing these things? Probably about as successful as my student was writing her kitten piece.

Another problem I experienced with using webs for prewriting was that students seemed to ignore them when they began to write. In translating their web ideas into a multi-paragraph essay or report, at least half the ideas always seemed to get left behind. At other times ideas would wind up in the writing that never appeared on the web to begin with. In other words, many students did not translate web material to the writing it was supposed to enhance. It was as though they never made the connection that the web was a means to an end and not an end in itself.

I had to conclude that a web was not a useful prewriting tool for students. It was fine for semantic mapping and brainstorming, even for note-taking, but as a blueprint for expository writing it was a poor choice.

The Advantages of the "Expository Pillar"

So, if my tried-and-true web wasn't going to work, what would? What kind of blueprint, framework, or graphic organizer would help my students organize their expository writing? I figured that two heads are better than one. So, during a get-away weekend in Stratton, Vermont, I sat down with my colleague Dea Paoletta Auray to talk about this. We worked for a long time and, after arguing, revising, and quite a bit of laughing, finally came up with a more helpful organizational prewriting framework. We called it the Expository Pillar.

There are many benefits to using this graphic organizer rather than a web:

1. It is sequential, moving from top to bottom, left to right, just like a piece of writing. The introduction and conclusion are the broadest parts, balancing one another at the top and the bottom (beginning and ending), giving the overall structure symmetry. The body of the piece, containing the three main ideas, is divided into paragraphs, with each main idea broader than the related details that support it.

2. It works regardless of the piece's length. Whether there are three paragraphs in the body of the piece, or twenty, the pillar can be adjusted and still stand firm because the broad introduction and conclusion, as well as the anchoring main ideas, remain solid and in proportion.

3. It can help students determine whether they have enough information (details) to support a main idea. If the student who wrote the kitten piece, for example, had applied her ideas to the Expository Pillar, she would have realized right away that she did not have the minimum number of supporting details, four, to fully support each main idea. At that point, the student could have eliminated those main ideas or done more research to dig up more supporting details to construct a well-elaborated paragraph. So, the Expository Pillar not only helps students organize information effectively but also reveals whether they have sufficient information to support their initial ideas.

| **Introduction** |
| (Lead and Thesis Statement) |

Main Idea #1	
Detail	Detail
Detail	Detail

Main Idea #2	
Detail	Detail
Detail	Detail

Main Idea #3	
Detail	Detail
Detail	Detail

| **Conclusion** |
| (Creatively Restated Main Ideas) |

The Expository Pillar: A powerful graphic organizer.

Of course, it is unrealistic to expect students to review the Expository Pillar and build a piece around it. They need to be introduced to the pillar, analyze pieces of expository writing that started from it (as well as some that weren't, for comparison), and then begin to use the pillar to build their own pieces. Use the reproducible on the next page for analyzing published pieces or planning original ones.

Over the years, I have created succinct, expository pieces on many topics that relate to our curriculum and school culture. Here is a partial list of topics:

The Saltmarsh and Seashore	Phys-ed Class
Abraham Lincoln	Presidents' Day
Immigration	Chinese New Year
The Rainforest	Thanksgiving
Martin Luther King, Jr.	Veterans' Day
Owls	Autumn-Winter—changes in nature
Eggs	The Woodland Habitat
Whales	Springtime—changes in nature

Name _____ Date _____

Introduction
(Lead and Thesis Statement)

_____

_____

Main Idea #1 _____

Detail _____	Detail _____
_____	_____
Detail _____	Detail _____
_____	_____

Main Idea #2 _____

Detail _____	Detail _____
_____	_____
Detail _____	Detail _____
_____	_____

Main Idea #3 _____

Detail _____	Detail _____
_____	_____
Detail _____	Detail _____
_____	_____

Conclusion
(Creatively Restated Main Ideas)

_____

_____

Analyze and Diagram a Piece of Expository Writing

This lesson will help your students understand the organization of a piece of expository writing.

1. I make a transparency of the piece "Thanksgiving" on page 29, for use on the overhead.

2. I make photocopies of the piece and the Diagramming Questions on page 30 for each child.

3. I explain to students that we will be analyzing and diagramming the piece together.

4. I read the piece aloud, beginning to end, asking students to follow along.

5. I go back and talk through the piece with students, paragraph by paragraph, diagramming all key sections on the overhead, using the question sheet as a guide.

As I read the piece aloud, I emphasize the way each detail sentence within the paragraph supports the main idea. For example, I might say, "Let's read paragraph two. Here's the main-idea sentence: 'Do you know the history of Thanksgiving in America?' Underline that main idea."

The students underline the sentence on their photocopies, as I do the same on the transparency. "Now, in a word—or a *blurb*—what will this entire paragraph be about?"

"History" one student says.

I write "history" in the margin beside the paragraph. Then I go on reading: 'It began in the times of the Pilgrims.' Is that about the history of Thanksgiving?"

"Yes," they reply.

I go on. "'After surviving the long voyage to America and the first harsh winter, the Pilgrims planned a feast.' Is that about the history of Thanksgiving?"

"Uh huh," they mumble.

"'Their Native American neighbors were invited to join in giving thanks and celebrating.' Is that about the history of Thanksgiving?"

"Yes," they say, perturbed that I'm repeating myself, but they get the point.

I proceed in similar fashion through the rest of the paragraph, matching each and every detail sentence with the main idea: History of Thanksgiving.

This line of questioning may seem rather dull and predictable, and for some students it is. But for many it leads to an important revelation: each and every detail sentence in a paragraph must support the main idea.

I want my students to be asking themselves questions like these about each paragraph they write, as a personal guide for relevance, elaboration, and tight organization.

Topic, Title

introduction

(Thanksgiving)

lead: a question

1. Did you know that most countries around the world set aside a special holiday for people to reflect and give thanks for the good things they've received throughout the year? The United States is no different. Each year, on the third Thursday of November we celebrate the holiday we call Thanksgiving. *thesis statement*

history

2. Do you know the history of Thanksgiving in America? It began in the times of the Pilgrims! After surviving the long voyage to America and the first harsh winter the Pilgrims planned a feast. Their Native American neighbors were invited to join in giving thanks and celebrating. Wild turkeys and deer were roasted, oysters were steamed, and fruits and vegetables were prepared. The festival lasted several days! Outdoor games were played. People took a break from the difficult daily work that was necessary to survive in this new land. This began the traditional celebration we know as Thanksgiving.

traditions

3. Nowadays there are new and different Thanksgiving traditions. When we think of Thanksgiving we think of football. High schools and colleges nation-wide play one of their biggest games of the season on Thanksgiving Day. Thousands of fans brave cold weather to go out and cheer them on. Millions watch professional football on T.V. after their Thanksgiving dinners. Another tradition is the Macy's Thanksgiving Day Parade! Marching bands, floats, and giant balloons make their way down Broadway in New York City. There are clowns and people on horseback. The air is filled with music and excitement as the parade passes by!

food

4. Of course, the best part about Thanksgiving is the food! The traditional modern American feast includes roast, stuffed turkey. Most people have mashed potatoes and gravy, cranberry sauce, plenty of vegetables, sweet potatoes, and pumpkin pie. Every family adds their own special touches to the menu. Some might have a pasta dish, others may enjoy a vegetarian variation. Most towns also give thanks by providing a feast for the poor and the homeless, so that everyone can enjoy the day.

5. So, as November rolls around we begin to reflect on the wonderful Thanksgiving holiday--its rich history, *main idea #1* its enjoyable traditional activities, *main idea #2* and most of all, the feast with family and friends. *main idea #3* It is certainly a special time to be thankful for the many good things we have received throughout the year! *conclusion*

> *Diagramming essays as a class helps students see how expository pieces are organized.*

Thanksgiving

Did you know that most countries around the world set aside a special holiday for people to reflect and give thanks for the good things they've received throughout the year? The United States is no different. Each year, on the third Thursday of November we celebrate the holiday we call Thanksgiving.

Do you know the history of Thanksgiving in America? It began in the times of the Pilgrims. After surviving the long voyage to America and the first harsh winter, the Pilgrims planned a feast. Their Native American neighbors were invited to join in giving thanks and celebrating. Wild turkeys and deer were roasted, oysters were steamed, and fruits and vegetables were prepared. The festival lasted several days. Outdoor games were played. People took a break from the difficult daily work that was necessary to survive in this new land. This began the traditional celebration we know as Thanksgiving.

Nowadays there are new and different Thanksgiving traditions. When we think of Thanksgiving we think of football. High schools and colleges nation-wide play one of their biggest games of the season on Thanksgiving Day. Thousands of fans brave cold weather to go out and cheer them on. Millions watch professional football on T.V. after their Thanksgiving dinners. Another tradition is the Macy's Thanksgiving Day Parade. Marching bands, floats, and giant balloons make their way down Broadway in New York City. There are clowns and people on horseback. The air is filled with music and excitement as the parade passes by!

Of course, the best part about Thanksgiving is the food! The traditional modern American feast includes roast, stuffed turkey. Most people have mashed potatoes and gravy, cranberry sauce, plenty of vegetables, sweet potatoes, and pumpkin pie. Every family adds their own special touches to the menu. Some might have a pasta dish, others may enjoy a vegetarian variation. Most towns also give thanks by providing a feast for the poor and the homeless, so that everyone can enjoy the day.

So, as November rolls around, we begin to reflect on the wonderful Thanksgiving holiday—its rich history, its enjoyable traditional activities, and most of all, the feast with family and friends. It is certainly a special time to be thankful for the many good things we have received throughout the year!

"*Thanksgiving*" *Diagramming Questions*

1. Read the title. What is the topic of this piece?

2. Number each paragraph.

3. Circle the introduction paragraph. Box the conclusion paragraph.

4. Look at paragraphs 2, 3, and 4 in the body of the piece. Underline each main idea sentence that tells what the entire paragraph is about. Write a word in the margin (a blurb) that sums up the main idea.

5. If you wanted to go back and find out about a modern day Thanksgiving tradition, which paragraph would you reread? _____

6. If you wanted to review the history of Thanksgiving, which paragraph would you read? _____

7. If you wanted to refer back to the foods of Thanksgiving, which paragraph would you read? _____

8. If the author wanted to add this detail to the piece: Some people serve apple pie for dessert. Where would it belong? paragraph #_____

9. If the author wanted to add this detail to the piece: The Native Americans performed special dances. Where would it belong? paragraph #_____

10. If the author wanted to add this detail to the piece: After Thanksgiving comes Christmas. Where would it belong? paragraph #_____

11. If the author wanted to add this detail to the piece: We have a parade on St. Patrick's Day too! Where would it belong? paragraph #_____

12. Fill in this summary:

This piece gives information about: _____.
Topic

The author EXPLAINS _____.
Main Idea #1

The author DISCUSSES _____.
Main Idea #2

The author DESCRIBES _____.
Main Idea #3

"Cut and Paste" Your Way to Good Organization

Once your students are familiar with analyzing the organization of a typical expository piece, try the diagramming lesson above using the now-famous kitten piece on page 20, to prepare them for the lesson that follows. Most likely, your students will easily identify the topic and number the paragraphs. But watch what happens when you ask them to underline each main idea and match it to a detail sentence. They will quickly realize that the piece is totally disorganized. Once they've made that discovery, try this lesson to show them how to create an organizational plan for the piece.

1. Before class, I reconfigure the kitten piece on the computer, sorting each detail sentence into three main-idea categories: Playful, Cute, and Easy to Own.

Playful

They are really playful when they chase a ball of string.
I would buy my kitten a stuffed mouse, some catnip, and many more fun toys.
They pretend to stalk things like your foot, and then they pounce.

Cute

They are really cute too.
They are small and furry and come in many different colors.
My Grandma's kitten is named Taffy because she is a brownish taffy color.
I would pick a kitten with green eyes.

Easy to Own

It is easy to get a kitten cause they don't cost a lot.
You can find an ad in the paper for free kittens or even a sign on a telephone
    pole right near your house.
They don't need to be walked like a dog does.
You'll need a litter box so they don't make a mess (if you know what I mean).
A scratching post is important so that your kitten won't ruin the furniture.
Kittens need shots from the vet so they won't get sick.

2. I print out each detail sentence in a large font size—large enough for students to read at a distance—and cut them into strips. Or you can hand print each sentence onto a strip.

3. I explain to the class that we are going to revise and reorganize the kitten piece.

4. On chart paper, I write a new introduction based on the ideas in the original piece:

> *Introduction:*
> *Can you imagine a pet that's soft and fluffy, playful and funny, adorable and easy to own? Of course, I'm talking about kittens! Kittens make the best possible pets.*

"Here's my revised introduction," I tell the students. "It gives the audience a better idea of the slant, tone, and main ideas the writer wants to present." I tape the chart paper to the chalkboard.

5. I go on, referring to the original piece. "It seems to me that the writer had a number of main ideas in mind. Can anybody pick them out?" The students discuss possibilities, and I eventually help them narrow their responses to the three main ideas: "cute" (appearance), "playful," and "easy to own." At the tops of three separate sheets of chart paper, which I line up next to the introduction chart, I translate each of these main-idea blurbs into a main-idea sentence:

> *Main Idea #1: Most people love kittens because they are so cute!*
> *Main Idea #2: Kittens are fun to have because they are so playful!*

Then I ask, "Can anyone help me come up with a main-idea sentence for the third blurb, 'easy to own'?"

The children call out a few ideas. I shape their responses into a good sentence, which I write on the fourth piece of chart paper:

> *Main Idea #3: It is certainly easy to acquire and care for a kitten.*

6. I go on to write a conclusion on a fifth piece of chart paper, and I tell the students, "Here's my revised conclusion that sums up each of the main ideas for the reader."

> *Conclusion:*
> *What could be cuter, more playful, or easier to own and care for than a kitten? It makes me wonder why anyone would want any other kind of pet!*

7. I explain that I have reproduced each of the writer's original detail sentences on separate strips of paper. (A reproducible set of these detail-sentence strips appears on page 34. Enlarge them on the photocopier and cut on the dotted lines.) I distribute the strips randomly to individuals or groups of students. Their task is to read the detail and decide under which main-idea category it belongs.

Introduction:

Can you imagine a pet that's soft and fluffy, playful and funny, adorable and easy to own? Of course, I'm talking about kittens! Kittens make the best possible pets.

Main Idea #1: Most people love kittens because they are so cute!

They are small and furry and come in many different colors.

My Grandma's kitten is named Taffy because she is a brownish taffy color.

I would pick a kitten with green eyes.

Main Idea #2: Kittens are fun to have because they are so playful!

They are really playful when they chase a ball of string.

They pretend to stalk things like your foot, and then they pounce.

I would buy my kitten a stuffed mouse, some catnip, and many more fun toys.

Main Idea #3: It is certainly easy to acquire and care for a kitten.

It is easy to get a kitten cause they don't cost a lot.

You can find an add in the paper for free kittens or even a sign on a telephone pole right near your house.

They don't need to be walked like a dog does.

You'll need a litter box so they don't make a mess (if you know what I mean).

Kittens need shots from the vet so they won't get sick.

A scratching post is important so that your kitten won't ruin the furniture.

Conclusion:

What could be cuter, more playful, or easier to own and care for than a kitten? It makes me wonder why anyone would want any other kind of pet!

Organizing details into categories— or main ideas—reinforces the importance of structure.

They are really playful when they chase a ball of string.

They are really cute too.

They don't need to be walked like a dog does.

They are small and furry and come in
many different colors.

It is easy to get a kitten cause they don't cost a lot.

You'll need a litter box so they don't make a mess
(if you know what I mean).

My Grandma's kitten is named Taffy because
she is a brownish taffy color.

I would pick a kitten with green eyes.

I would buy my kitten a stuffed mouse,
some catnip, and many more fun toys.

A scratching post is important so that
your kitten won't ruin the furniture.

You can find an ad in the paper for free kittens or even
a sign on a telephone post right near your house.

They pretend to stalk things like your foot,
and then they pounce.

Kittens need shots from the vet so they won't get sick.

8. After they've chosen a category, I ask students to bring their sentence strips up to the appropriate chart.

9. Using tape or glue sticks, students affix their sentences to the charts in some logical order. For example, in the "easy to own" category, they may feel it makes sense to mention first the fact that kittens don't need to be walked as dogs do and follow that with the litter box suggestion. It will look like the sentences on page 33.

10. I conclude the lesson by reading aloud their revised piece and comparing it with the earlier version. A sample revised piece follows. Notice how I highlighted the main-idea sentences and blurbs to reinforce their importance:

Kittens

Can you imagine a pet that's soft and fluffy, playful and funny, adorable and easy to own? Of course, I'm talking about kittens! Kittens make the best possible pets.

<u>Most people love kittens because they are so **cute**!</u> They are small and furry and come in many different colors. My Grandma's kitten is named Taffy because she is a brownish taffy color. I would pick a kitten with green eyes.

<u>Kittens are fun to have because they are so **playful**!</u> They pretend to stalk things like your foot, and then they pounce. I would buy my kitten a stuffed mouse, some catnip, and many more fun toys. They are really playful when they chase a ball of string.

<u>It is certainly **easy to acquire and care for** a kitten.</u> It is easy to get a kitten because they don't cost a lot. You can find an ad in the paper for free kittens or even a sign on a telephone pole right near your house. They don't need to be walked like a dog does. You'll need a litter box so they don't make a mess (if you know what I mean). A scratching post is important so that your kitten won't ruin the furniture. Kittens need shots from the vet so they won't get sick.

What could be cuter, more playful, or easier to own than a kitten? It makes me wonder why anyone would want any other kind of pet!

This reorganized piece could now be easily diagrammed. On another day, follow this procedure with your class:

1. Number each paragraph.

2. Circle the introduction.

3. Box the conclusion.

4. Next to paragraphs 2, 3, and 4, underline the main idea sentences and write a blurb in the margin that tells what the entire paragraph is about.

5. Fill in this summary:

This piece gives information about: _____ .
Topic

The author DESCRIBES _____ .
Main Idea #1

The author DISCUSSES _____ .
Main Idea #2

The author EXPLAINS _____ .
Main Idea #3

Improving Sentence Variety and Adding Detail

Of course, while the reorganized piece is greatly improved, it is still a little stilted in terms of sentence variety. You can show students how to revise by adding a few transitional words and phrases, inserting or substituting some active verbs, providing vivid adjectives, and adding prepositional phrases.

Also, if students compare the piece with the Expository Pillar, they will see that some main ideas are not well supported. This is a great opportunity to have them brainstorm to generate additional detail sentences to support each main idea. (See Chapters 5 and 6 for more on generating powerful details.)

On the next page is a sample of how the final, revised piece might read. All revisions are indicated in boldfaced print.

Finally, read aloud the original stream-of-consciousness kitten piece, the cut-and-pasted version, and the final revised piece. Then ask your students:

♦ Which piece gives you the most information?

♦ Which piece makes the information easiest to find and understand?

♦ Which piece paints the clearest picture of kittens?

♦ They should recognize that, to be effective, expository pieces need to be well organized, fluent, and fully elaborated.

Kittens

· · · · · · · ·

Can you imagine a pet that's soft and fluffy, playful and funny, adorable and easy to own? Of course, I'm talking about kittens! Kittens make the best possible pets.

Most people love kittens because they are so cute! They are small and furry and come in many different colors. For example, my Grandma's kitten is named Taffy because she is a brownish taffy color. You might choose a kitten in gray or black , orange or white. There are tabbies and stripes and calico kittens as well! You will melt when you look into the sweet eyes of a kitten! I would pick a kitten with bright green eyes. Some kittens also have sapphire blue eyes and even golden eyes!

Kittens are fun to have because they are so playful! They pretend to stalk things like your foot, and then they pounce. I would buy my kitten a gray furry stuffed mouse, some catnip in a small felt pouch, and a small rubber ball that squeaks. Have you ever seen a kitten chase a ball of string? They run this way and that, batting it with their tiny paws, chasing it across the floor and beneath furniture.

It is certainly easy to acquire and care for a kitten. You might be surprised to learn that kittens don't usually cost a lot. You can often find an ad in the paper for free kittens or even a hand-printed sign on a telephone pole right near your house. And do you realize that kittens and cats don't need to be walked like a dog does? However, you'll need a litter box and plenty of kitty litter so they don't make a mess on the floor (if you know what I mean). Since kittens love to flex their claws and scratch, a sturdy scratching post is important. This way your kitten won't ruin the furniture. Of course, keep in mind that kittens need shots from the vet so they won't get sick.

What could be cuter, more playful, or easier to own than a kitten? It makes me wonder why anyone would want any other kind of pet!

Making the Jump from Analyzing a Plan to Creating One

After all this analysis, diagramming, and cutting and pasting, your students will begin to understand the organizational pattern of expository writing—and can begin applying these ideas to their own writing.

However, making the jump from analyzing someone else's blueprint to creating your own from scratch isn't easy. It's a little like the difference between a carpenter and an architect. A carpenter can recognize and follow a great set of plans and maybe revise a poor one to make it work. But the architect creates an effective, workable plan from scratch.

At this point, your students may be expository "carpenter apprentices." With a little guidance, they can critique and follow another's plan. In the next chapter we will begin the work of creating "architects"—students who can plan, design, and apply what they know to their own writing.

Create a Classroom Chart of Transitional Phrases

With the help of your students, you might want to maintain a classroom chart of transitional phrases to use as reference. Start with the ones inserted into the kitten piece revision:

For example…

Can you imagine…?

Have you ever seen…?

You might be surprised to learn that…

And do you realize that…?

However…

Since…

This way…

Of course, keep in mind that…

Chapter 3

Creating a Prewriting Plan

Identifying Broad—Yet Distinct—Main Ideas

I f you carry out all the diagramming, discussing, and dissecting I've described to this point, your students should have a good grasp of the organizational framework of expository writing. And, of course, with all that preliminary work under their belts, they should be ready to write a successful expository piece, right?

Wrong, if your students are like mine.

The Dog Piece

I'd spent almost two months with fifth-grade students, immersed in the kind of work I shared with you in previous chapters. We'd thoroughly analyzed the kitten piece. They got it. Honestly, all of them got it. So, I decided to assign a piece of writing that I thought would be easy for them—a parallel topic that would translate easily: dogs. I knew that all of my students had some first-hand experience with dogs. So I seized the opportunity to take what they had learned from the kitten piece and rehash it with a slightly different slant. Simple, right?

Wrong again.

I began by reminding them what they'd learned. We reviewed the Expository Pillar described on page 25, and I distributed a prewriting planner that contained major components of the pillar:

TOPIC: Dogs
Main Idea #1:
Main Idea #2:
Main Idea #3:

My students filled in their planners and started writing. I reminded them that they needed an introduction that addressed their three main ideas. I reminded them that each detail sentence must support the main idea: "Does *this* belong . . . ? Does *that* belong . . . ? Is *this* about your main idea . . . ? Is *that* about your main idea?" They knew the mantra by heart and applied it as they worked, doing their best to keep only relevant details in each paragraph. I reminded them that their conclusion paragraph must sum up what came before. I was confident that my students knew all of this and that my reminders served simply as reinforcers. They continued to work, pencils scribbling away, tongues peeking out from the corners of their mouths, reading their words over and over silently, checking their planners as they went, just as they'd been taught to do.

Let me share one child's piece on the next page.

As I assess this piece, in fairness to the student, I focus only on what I have taught thus far. I look only at organization—at how the student arranged the information she wanted to share. I am not concerned, at this point, with word choice, sentence variety, or the quality of supporting details. Specifically, I ask myself:

- ♦ **Is there a clear introduction paragraph that tells what the entire piece will be about?** Yes. The student gives the reader the topic, dogs, as well as the three main ideas: dogs are playful, friendly, and good company.

- ♦ **Does each detail support the main idea in the paragraph?** Yes. If you go through each paragraph and ask, "Does *this* belong . . . ? Does *that* belong . . . ?" you will find that each detail sentence "fits" sensibly in its paragraph.

Dogs

If I could have any pet in the pet store I would have a dog. I would like to have a dog because dogs are playful, they are friendly, and they will keep you company.

My first reason I would like to have a dog is because he will keep me company. My dog would go on walks with me every day. We would play Frisbee in my yard. We could also play tug-of-war with a stick. This is a good thing because when I have no one to play with he will be ready.

My second reason that I would want to have a dog is because he will spend time with me and play with me. When I am lonely he will always be there for me, ready to play. When I am sad he will cheer me up by bringing me a stick to throw. And when I have nothing to do he will make me take him for a walk maybe. I would love for him to do this.

My last reason that I would want a dog is because he will be my friend. My dog will protect me and will never hurt me. And in return I will be nice to him. Give him a Milk Bone. Play with him more. We would be friends.

So now I hope you can see why I would want a dog. He is playful, friendly, and would keep me company. After all, a dog is man's best friend. Oh, and by the way, I would name him Alex.

Intro:
main ideas:
1. playful
2. friendly
3. keep you company

Good ideas—now let's work on making sure they don't overlap!

Dogs

If I could have any pet in the store I would have a dog. I would like to have a dog because dogs are playful, they are friendly, and they will keep you company.

My first reason I would like to have a dog is because he will keep me company. My dog would go on walks with me everyday. We would play frisbee in my yard. We could also play tug-of-war with a stick. This is a good thing because when I have no one to play with he will be ready.

My second reason that I would want a dog is because he will spend time with me and play with me. When I am lonely he will always be there for me, ready to play. When I am sad he will cheer me up by bringing me a stick to throw. And when I have nothing to do he will make me take him for a walk maybe. I would love for him to do this. My last reason I would want a dog is because he will be my friend. My dog will protect me and never hurt me. And in return I will be nice to him. Give him a milk bone. Play with him more. We would be friends.

So now I hope you can see why I would want a dog. He is playful, friendly, and would keep me company. After all a dog is a mans best friend. Oh, and by the way, I would name him Alex.

Is this all about keeping company, or about playing?

Spending time, keeping company, or playing?

Hmm . . . About being friendly—or about playing?

The original dog piece with teacher comments.

41

♦ **Is there a conclusion paragraph that "sums up" the piece by restating the main ideas?** Yes. The three main ideas—playful, friendly, and good company—are restated in the last paragraph.

I nibble my lip and frown. The student did do all of the things I suggested. The paper passed my check system. But still, I wasn't satisfied with it. The writing seemed overly general—a problem that somehow went deeper than verbs, adjectives, and details.

I read several other papers and was struck by similar feelings. The work lacked depth . . . "Dogs are nice," "Dogs are fun," "I like dogs." I knew instinctively that the problem was related to organization, despite accurate paragraphing, but I was not clear exactly what it was.

I read and reread my students' pieces, looking for an answer. But I didn't find it until I went back to the prewriting planner of the student who wrote the dog piece on page 41:

TOPIC: Dogs
Main Idea #1:   Keep me company
Main Idea #2:   Spend time with me/play with me
Main Idea #3:   Be my friend

Then, I assigned a blurb to each main idea (i.e. Company, Spend Time/Play, and Friendly), made a list of each detail sentence, and did an imaginary cut-and-paste lesson. My list of detail sentences follows. Read it over and try to assign each sentence to the correct blurb.

Dog Piece Detail Sentences

My dog would go on walks with me every day.
We would play Frisbee in my yard.
We could also play tug-of-war with a stick.
This is a good thing because when I have no one to play with he will be ready.
When I am lonely he will always be there for me, ready to play.
When I am sad he will cheer me up by bringing me a stick to throw.
And when I have nothing to do he will make me take him for a walk maybe. I
     would love him to do this.
My dog will protect me and will never hurt me.
And in return I will be nice to him. Give him a Milk Bone. Play with him more.
     We would be friends.

Did you "paste" each detail to a main idea? What did you discover? Let's look at a few of the detail sentences again and assign each one to main idea 1, 2, or 3:

"We would play Frisbee in my yard."

Would that sentence best support Company, Spend Time/Play, or Friendly? The fact is, it could support any of them! "Playing Frisbee" is one way a dog might keep you company. It is certainly a way to play and spend time with a dog. And it is an expression of "friendship" between a dog and a person.

How about this one:

"When I am lonely he will always be there for me, ready to play."

Again, this detail represents playing, keeping company, and being friends with a dog. So where does it belong?

What the Dog Piece Taught Me:
The Importance of Broad, Yet Distinct, Main Ideas

It was completely clear that most of the detail sentences in the dog piece could fit into more than one paragraph. The main ideas were so similar that the details supporting them were almost interchangeable. This is precisely why this piece and others had an overly general feeling to them.

That was a big "a-ha" moment for me. I realized that for a piece to really work, each main idea must be distinct from other main ideas in the piece, yet be broad enough to support a number of details. When main ideas overlap, the details also tend to overlap and become redundant and random.

Identifying Overlapping Main Ideas

So my mission became to teach my students how to construct broad, yet distinct, main-idea sentences. I started by asking students to look closely at each main-idea blurb in their prewriting planners for their dog pieces. Then, I had them look closely at their detail sentences. If a detail could fit into more than one paragraph, that would be a signal telling them that the main ideas were not distinct enough from one another. From there, I devised a number of activities that would help my students use this procedure consistently.

Determine if the Main Ideas Are Distinct

I present my students with a sample prewriting planner for a piece on boating, along with some detail sentences:

TOPIC: Boating
Main Idea #1: Fun
Main Idea #2: Exciting
Main Idea #3: Cool Hobby

It is really fun to hoist the sails and start sailing over the open sea.
It is cool to take your gear out on the boat for some fishing fun.
Passing other boaters speeding by is another reason I love boating.

I ask them to place numbers beside each detail sentence, indicating where it might belong in the piece of writing—1 for Main Idea #1, 2 for Main Idea #2, and 3 for Main Idea #3. Here's a typical response:

It is really fun to hoist the sails and start sailing over the open sea. # 1, 2
It is cool to take your gear out on the boat for some fishing fun. # 3, 1
Passing other boaters speeding by is another reason I love boating. #1, 2, 3

Finally, I ask them what they notice. As soon as they see that details are fitting into more than one paragraph, they realize that the main idea sentences overlap—and, therefore, are not distinct enough from one another to create a successful piece of writing. On the next page, you will find several more reproducible examples of this activity.

Name _____ Date _____

$\mathcal{D}$o the Main Ideas Overlap?

Directions: Match the main ideas in each prewriting planner to the detail sentences that follow. Are the main ideas distinct enough from one another?

Prewriting Planner:

TOPIC: My Grandmother

Main Idea #1: Fun to Be With

Main Idea #2: Nice

Main Idea #3: Cares About Me

Detail Sentences:

My Grandmother helps me bake cookies with her. Main Idea # _____

She lets me sleep over in her beautiful spare room. Main Idea # _____

When I'm sick she'll come over to watch me and do jigsaw puzzles together.

Main Idea # _____

Are the main ideas distinct enough from one another? Yes No

Prewriting Planner:

TOPIC: Terrific Franklin School

Main Idea #1: The Best Teachers

Main Idea #2: Brand New Playground

Main Idea #3: The Franklin School Spring Fair

Detail Sentences:

Each classroom sponsors a game at the fair. Main Idea # _____

Our teachers are kind, but they're sort of strict, too, in a good way. _____

Main Idea # _____

The PTA built all of the new playground equipment. Main Idea # _____

Are the main ideas distinct enough from one another? Yes No

Separating Overlapping Main Ideas

As often happens in teaching, there's a sense of excitement when you've finally gotten to the bottom of a challenge, and then there's the letdown. Now that you know the problem, what can you do about it?

My students began to distinguish between distinct and overlapping main ideas, but they were often stumped about how to "fix" overlapping ones. So I spoke to other teachers about it. "You're really talking about something much broader than writing," said one seasoned colleague. "You're talking about thinking—doing pretty sophisticated critical thinking."

I nodded.

Another teacher with particular expertise in science and math, piped in. "We do this stuff in first grade," she said. "We call it sorting and categorizing. We talk about Venn diagrams, the ways in which things relate to one another, what they have in common, how they're different."

She was right. I could see what she was getting at. Being able to see the ways ideas overlapped or differed from one another was essentially what my students needed. So I needed to present them with some activities that would enable them to think critically about ideas, in ways they had in their earlier years at school.

The first-grade teacher watched my eyes light up and gave me the thumbs-up sign. As I do whenever I need to clarify my thinking, I went to my grade partner, Dea Auray, and we figured out how to make this concept clear for our students. Dea came up with our favorite categorizing lesson, "Pick, List, and Choose."

Lesson:
Categorize Main Ideas with "Pick, List, and Choose"

This whole-class lesson is easy, fun, and serves a number of purposes. It relates directly to the organizational strategies necessary for good writing, builds critical-thinking skills, and reinforces curriculum content. It can be done in 10 minutes and is a valuable way to use up "dead time" in your day—those moments between returning from gym and leaving for lunch, for example. Essentially, what you do is spread a whole pile of "detail bricks" across the floor and have students sort them into categories—much as first graders do with attribute blocks for learning size, shape, and color.

1. Pick: I gather the class around a flip chart or the blackboard and introduce the lesson with a topic that my students are all familiar with, such as autumn.

"I've picked a topic that we all know a lot about." I write "Autumn" on the chart. "Autumn is a terrific time of year. Besides being beautiful, it's a season in which many changes take place—changes in the weather, in nature, in activities we take part in."

2. **List:** I've got their attention, and a student or two throws out some thoughts. "There's Halloween," says one. "I love Halloween." Others nod in agreement. "And the leaves change color," adds another student.

"Hold those thoughts for a minute," I say. "We're going to list everything we know about autumn on this chart. You call out to me what is important or unique about autumn, and I'll list your ideas as quickly as I can."

They don't give me a second to catch my breath. The ideas strike like machine-gun fire: "Halloween!" "Shorter days!" "Birds migrating!" "Squirrels gathering nuts!" "Thanksgiving!" "Football!" "Raking leaves!"

"Okay, hold on," I beg. "Let me catch up." I scribble frantically, listing their ideas. One student's contribution inspires others. Our list looks like the one to the right.

"That's a long list," I say, nodding my head and smiling. They are grasping for additional ideas, eager to keep me hopping.

"Going to the mall," Gayle shouts. I pause, marker poised in the air. "Hmmm . . ." I say, "I'm not as sure about that . . . ."

Gayle rushes on, "My aunt and I always go to the mall together and I know she'll probably take me before fall is over."

"Yeah, but that could happen any time of year," says Dan.

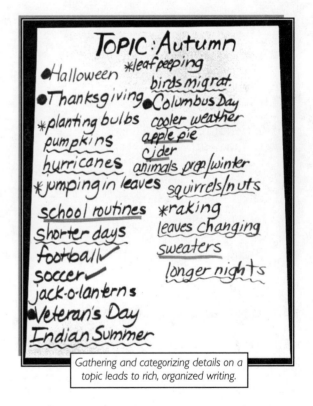

Gathering and categorizing details on a topic leads to rich, organized writing.

"Doesn't belong," agrees Jessie. "Mrs. Mariconda said it should be unique to autumn."

"What do you think?" I ask the rest of them.

"Well," says Katie, always the peacemaker, "It might work in a list called, 'Autumn with Gayle,' but not in a list called just plain 'Autumn'."

The students nod, and Gayle seems okay with that.

3. Choose: I step back and look at the list. "Here's what we've done so far. I took a moment to pick a topic, autumn. We made a list of details about autumn. Now we are going to choose some main ideas that will organize the details you gave me."

We look again at the list and try to see if we can group the ideas by categories. "Okay," I say, "I'm looking at Halloween, Columbus Day, Veterans' Day, and Thanksgiving. What category do these belong in?"

"Holidays," someone shouts.

"Fall holidays," another offers.

I underline in red each fall holiday on our list. "Can anybody find another category or main idea?" I ask, carefully weaving in expository terminology.

"Sports," shouts Catherine. "Autumn sports!"

"Which ideas—*or details*—fall under autumn sports?" I ask.

A chorus of "football" and "soccer," with a few "leaf-peeping hikes" in the background, comes my way.

"Hmmm . . ." I say. "That's only two solid details, and one 'iffy' detail. That might not be enough to support a paragraph. What's a category that would definitely include football, soccer, and leaf-peeping hikes, as well as planting bulbs, raking leaves, and jumping in leaves?"

"Stuff to do outside!" Jeff yells.

Melanie cleans it up a little. "Outdoor autumn activities."

"Same thing," mutters Jeff.

I nod. "That's right. Sports might be too limiting, but if the main-idea category is outdoor activities, it would encompass all of these ideas." I underline all the outdoor activities in green.

"Give me another main-idea category," I say.

The students try out a number of ideas: "changes," "new season," "nature in autumn." They finally decide that hurricanes, cool weather, leaves changing, shorter days/longer nights, birds migrating, squirrels gathering nuts, Indian summer, and animals preparing for winter belong in a main idea category called "How autumn weather affects nature." I underline all of these ideas in blue.

We're left with the following details: pumpkins, jack-o-lanterns, school routines, apple pie, cider, and sweaters. "What do we do with these?" I ask.

"Maybe you include jack-o-lanterns with Halloween," Mark suggests. "And pumpkins with Thanksgiving."

"How about autumn food?" says Danny.

"Not enough food for that," says Carla, "unless you count pumpkins as a food, or add pumpkin pie to the list."

I sit back and let them talk.

"Sweaters can go with cooler weather," says Jon.

Karen sits up, suddenly excited. "How about 'How autumn weather affects people!" she squeals. "They buy pumpkins, carve jack-o-lanterns, get into school routines, wear sweaters, and eat apple pie!"

The others agree.

"And they drink cider too!" adds Peter.

"Excellent thinking!" I say, and begin underlining these last details in orange.

"So, let's choose our broad, yet distinct, main ideas." I transfer the information on the chart to a prewriting planner, which is now familiar to the children:

> TOPIC: Autumn
> Main Idea #1: How Autumn Weather
> Affects Nature
> Main Idea #2: How Autumn Weather Affects People
> Main Idea #3: Outdoor Autumn Activities

Pick, List , and Choose . . . at a Glance

1. PICK a familiar topic, one that your class knows plenty of details about.

2. LIST all the details they know. You may find that some "details" are actually broad enough to be a main idea. For example, if a student had said, "I love food we have in autumn." And another said, "I love cider and pumpkin pie," I would have written them all down. Later in the lesson, I make it clear that autumn foods encompass pumpkin pie and cider.

3. CHOOSE broad, yet distinct, main ideas to categorize the details. During this part add, delete, or combine details. After all, that is what authors do as they plan and write.

"Are these main ideas broad enough?" I ask. "In other words, do you have at least four supporting details for each of them?"

The students glance back at the chart and nod.

I go on. "Are these main ideas distinct enough? Do they overlap in any way?"

Kelly tips her head. "Not unless you're carving the jack-o-lantern outside." The children laugh.

"I think they're broad, yet distinct," I say. "These main ideas would help you organize our details well, for a great piece of writing."

"Pick, List, and Choose" Topics

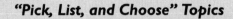

Here is a list of possible topics to use for the Pick, List, and Choose lesson. Refer to it when you need a topic or use it as a guide for coming up with topics of your own.

"Generic" Topics	Curriculum Related Topics
Winter	Rain Forest
Spring	Desert Habitat
Summer	Great Explorers
Halloween	Rev. Martin Luther King, Jr.
Thanksgiving	Abraham Lincoln
(or any other holiday you observe)	(or any other notable people you study)
Gym Class	Mars (or any planet)
Art Class	Your State (or any state)
Music Class	Immigration
Computer Lab	Seashore Habitat
Your School	The Civil War
The Playground	Westward Expansion
Your Cafeteria	Flight
A Field Trip You Went On	The Underground Railroad
A Favorite Teacher	A Foreign Country
Friendship	The Pilgrims
Your School Fair	An Animal You've Studied

Extending the Pick, List, and Choose Lesson

Pick, List, and Choose is most effective when it is repeated many times on different topics the students care about. Once your students are comfortable with the basic approach, assign three or four main ideas that you know overlap and let students figure it out for themselves. For example, for our autumn lesson, I might have created the following prewriting plan:

> TOPIC: Autumn
> Main Idea #1: Autumn Weather
> Main Idea #2: Things You See in Autumn
> Main Idea #3: Autumn Sports
> Main Idea #4: Things You Do in Autumn

Clearly, main ideas #1 and #2 could overlap. Leaves changing color result from weather changes and, of course, is something you can see. Main ideas #3 and #4 also overlap. Football, for example, is a sport as well as something you do in autumn. Because the main ideas are not distinct enough from one another, my students would, I hope, decide that this prewriting plan would be ineffective.

A number of simple prewriting plans follow. After your students have had sufficient experience "picking, listing, and choosing" with you, have them discuss the quality of each plan. Encourage them to pick out main ideas that overlap, as well as those that are too narrow— those from which they would be hard-pressed to generate at least four related supporting details. And remember, this is a thinking exercise. Students do not need to use these plans as starting points for their own writing. The answers to the practice sheet examples are:
1. This plan works! 2. #1 and #3 overlap. 3. This plan works! 4. #1 and #2 overlap! #2 is too narrow. 5. This plan works! 6. Almost all main ideas overlap!

Name _____ Date _____

$\mathcal{D}$o the Plans Work?

Directions: Do these prewriting plans work . . . or do the main ideas overlap too much?

1. TOPIC: The Beach

Main Idea #1: Seashore Creatures

Main Idea #2: Beach Gear You'll Need

Main Idea #3: Beach Activities

_____

_____

_____

2. TOPIC: Winter

Main Idea #1: Fun in the Snow

Main Idea #2: Winter Holidays

Main Idea #3: Skiing

_____

_____

_____

3. TOPIC: Abraham Lincoln

Main Idea #1: Early Life

Main Idea #2: Appearance

Main Idea #3: Adult Life

Main Idea #4: Influence on America

_____

_____

_____

4. TOPIC: Super Ice Cream Sundae

Main Idea #1: Ingredients

Main Idea #2: Whipped Cream

Main Idea #3: Where to Get One

_____

_____

_____

5. TOPIC: The Desert Habitat

Main Idea #1: Weather/Climate

Main Idea #2: Animals

Main Idea #3: Plants, Trees

_____

_____

_____

6. TOPIC: Ground Hog Day

Main Idea #1: Groundhog Day
           Traditions

Main Idea #2: Groundhog Facts

Main Idea #3: Groundhog Behavior

Main Idea #4: Why I Like
           Groundhog Day

_____

_____

_____

But, When Do They Get to Write?

You may be saying, "Okay, all of this is great, but shouldn't my students be writing?" Time spent conceptualizing, thinking, and planning is what prewriting is all about. And solid prewriting skills prevent a lot of the tedious, painful revisions that students so often resist.

To illustrate, let's go back to my kitchen renovation. I have to admit that it's frustrating being without a sink for a week and without a counter for a whole month. Nevertheless, during this time, our kitchen designer, carpenter, electrician, and plumber are working together to save headaches later. First it's framing, then the electrical work and plumbing, sheet rocking and taping, flooring, and finally, cabinetry. The time for discovering a misplaced pipe is not after the sheetrock and cabinetry are in place. Imagine having to tear out the cabinets and cut through the sheetrock to resolve this problem.

My point is that this time spent in the "thinking" phase is well worth it. In fact, it is a kind of virtual writing. In the next chapter, I will demonstrate how to help students use their effective, well-thought-through plans to begin constructing successful expository pieces.

Chapter 4

Putting the Plan into Action

Writing Broad–Yet Distinct–Main Ideas

We're finally ready to begin writing. My students have a thorough understanding of organization because we've studied the Expository Pillar, described on page 24. They can use the Pick, List, and Choose procedure described on page 46 to generate details on their topics and group them under broad, yet distinct, main ideas. Our next challenge is translating descriptive blurbs from our prewriting plans into well-constructed main-idea sentences.

𝒫owerful Main-Idea Sentences

We have been studying the estuary, learning much about the animals, birds, and insects that inhabit marshlands. I've chosen "Horseshoe Crabs" as my topic for a piece of expository writing. Using the Pick, List, and Choose procedure, my students help me sort through all the details about horseshoe crabs and group them into the following prewriting plan:

> TOPIC: Horseshoe Crabs
> Main Idea #1: Appearance
> Main Idea #2: Habitat
> Main Idea #3: Behavior

I put that prewriting plan on a chart, direct students' attention to the first main-idea blurb, "Appearance," and ask them how they might use it to introduce a paragraph. Often, they suggest simply plugging the blurb into the beginning of their paragraph, like this:

> Appearance. The horseshoe crab is covered with a thick reddish brown shell. It looks a little bit like a large helmet with a pointy straight tail.

This isn't surprising, considering magazine, textbook, and encyclopedia writers use headings like that to assist the reader in finding information quickly and easily.

However, in an essay, using the main-idea blurb as a heading is not appropriate. The blurb must be translated into a complete, well-constructed sentence. Further, main-idea sentences must be varied so that the piece overall doesn't sound like a broken record:

> Main Idea #1: First, I will tell you about the horseshoe crab's appearance.
> Main Idea #2: Next, I will tell you about where horseshoe crabs live.
> Main Idea #3: Finally, I will tell you about horseshoe crab behavior.

That said, it's never enough to tell students, "Don't use repetitive language." The fact is, if you take away something that they are comfortable doing, you must give them tools to use in its place. That's where word referents and sentence starters come in.

Word Referents and Sentence Starters: Antidotes to Repetitive Language

One of the easiest ways to help students with repetitive or redundant language is to brainstorm some word referents, or synonym phrases, for words they're overusing. In the example on page 55, for instance, I would encourage students to come up with all the different ways to say "horseshoe crab." Our list might look something like this:

HORSESHOE CRAB
hardy crustacean . . .
fascinating arthropod . . .
estuary dweller . . .
interesting creature . . .

Even the broken-record sentences sound better when I replace "horseshoe crab" with those phrases:

Main Idea #1: *First, I will tell you about this hardy crustacean's appearance.*
Main Idea #2: *Next, I will tell you about where this interesting creature lives.*
Main Idea #3: *Finally, I will tell you about this fascinating arthropod's behavior.*

But what about the parts that really make this piece sound like a broken record—the "I will tell you about" parts? For young writers, addressing an audience with the purpose of sharing information is a new experience. They are unfamiliar with the words and phrases they can use to lead readers to the information they have to share.

So, I begin by providing my students a menu of sentence starters that can introduce any number of main ideas. My list for the horseshoe crab piece might look like this:

Have you ever seen _____?

You may be surprised to learn _____.

Are you aware of _____?

It is interesting to learn about _____.

Most people are unfamiliar with _____.

Let's take a look at _____.

Brainstorming synonyms for topics and providing sentence starters are great ways to circumvent redundant language.

I don't insist that my students choose from this list, but it is there if needed. Using the list to model ways to mix and match word referents and sentence starters, I create main-idea sentences that might read like this:

> <u>Let's take a look</u> at these fascinating arthropods.
> <u>You may be surprised to learn that</u> these hardy crustaceans are found in estuaries all over the world.
> <u>Most people are unfamiliar with</u> the behavior of the horseshoe crab.
> <u>Have you ever seen</u> one of these fascinating creatures?
> <u>It is interesting to learn about</u> this estuary dweller's habitat.
> <u>Are you aware of the</u> unusual behavior of these interesting crabs?

Then we go back and compare these main-idea sentences to the list at the beginning of the chapter. What a difference!

Lesson:

Play the Synonymous-Phrase Game

A fun way to get students used to referring to their topic in a variety of ways is through the synonymous-phrase game. Here's how it works.

1. Before class, write a different topic on 8 to 12 index cards. Well-known people, places, and things work best. Here's a list I've used:

Michael Jordan	Washington, D.C.	Martin Luther King, Jr.
magician	tarantula	desert
blue whale	Antarctica	grizzly bear
George Washington	Corvette Stingray	ostrich

2. Divide the class into groups of up to three students and give each group a topic card. Ask them to brainstorm a list of synonymous words and phrases for their topics. (Some students might simply list adjectives, rather than nouns, which will not work. The phrase must be able to replace the topic word in a sentence and still make sense.)

3. Give groups plenty of time to work and circulate through the class, asking helpful questions. For example, if students are struggling with mule as a topic, you might ask, "What animal is closely related to a mule?" They might respond, "A horse." Encourage them to write, "This close relative of the horse . . ." Ask, "How might you describe a mule?" They might respond, "Long ears, stubborn, four-legged." Encourage them to write, "This stubborn, four-legged beast" or "This long-eared, stubborn animal."

4. After about 15 to 20 minutes, have a representative from each group read their words and phrases aloud, while the rest of the class tries to name their topic. For example, the student might ask his classmates to identify: "This symbol of freedom," "This New York Harbor monument," "This gift from the French people," "Lady Liberty," "Incredible tourist attraction," "This sign of hope for immigrants." Of course, he would be referring to the Statue of Liberty.

5. Once students get the hang of it, give them an index card whenever they begin to write on a topic. The synonymous-phrase game can help them get started.

Activity:

Construct Main-Idea Sentences

Providing students with opportunities to practice this skill is important. You can do that by giving them a number of simple prewriting plans and having them translate each main-idea blurb into a sentence, using the sentence starters on the next page. You can approach this activity in a number of ways:

1. Have students work independently on a single topic and then compare results.

2. Break the class into small groups and assign each one a different topic.

3. Let each student choose the topic that interests him or her most.

Whichever approach you take, be sure to have students brainstorm some word referents to use in place of their topic word. Here are some simple prewriting plans to start with:

TOPIC: Horseback Riding
Main Idea #1: Where to Learn
Main Idea #2: Equipment Needed
Main Idea #3: Good Exercise

Create a Classroom Chart of Main-Idea Sentence Starters

This is a great time to begin a classroom sentence-starter chart. On a large piece of chart paper, or on individual sentence strips, brainstorm ways to begin main-idea sentences. Have students not only come up with them themselves but also pick some out of magazine articles and books. As the list grows, they can begin playing with the language, mixing and matching phrases in creative ways. Display this chart for students to refer to and add to throughout the year. You can also photocopy and distribute the sample chart on the next page.

TOPIC: Gardening
Main Idea #1: Growing Vegetables
Main Idea #2: Growing Flowers
Main Idea #3: Growing Herbs

Main-Idea Sentence Starters

It is amazing to think about _____
Let me explain _____
You'll be excited to learn that _____
Do you realize that _____
Have you ever thought about _____
Have you ever wondered _____
Let me tell you about _____
Of course, most people agree that _____
Actually, _____
It is interesting to note that _____
In a funny sort of way _____
Surprisingly, _____
Nowadays _____
Usually, _____
It's incredible that _____
Most often _____
Now that _____
By the way _____
You'd better believe that _____
You'll soon see that _____
Don't you think that _____
Wouldn't you agree _____
Certainly, _____
Positively, _____
Normally, _____
Finally _____
Experts agree that _____
Let me fill you in on _____
There are many reasons why _____
There are many ways in which _____
Interestingly enough, _____
Let's take a look at _____
It all began when _____
Have you ever seen _____
It is fascinating to learn about _____
Amazingly, _____
Unquestionably, _____
Surely, _____
Typically, _____
In my experience _____

Would you believe that _____
So, what about _____
Incredibly, _____
It is true that _____
So, you want to understand how _____
Why do _____
How can _____
When do _____
Where can _____
How do(es) _____
Most people believe that _____
Of course, _____
For sure, _____
Often times _____
For years _____
Sometimes _____
Historically, _____
It's hard to believe, but _____
You will find that _____
You'll soon discover why/that _____
So, _____
No one will argue that _____
Without a doubt _____
Truly, _____
In the first place _____
Imagine _____
First of all _____
In many ways _____
So why is (are) _____
What's so great about _____
Suppose that you _____
Do you remember when _____
Try to visualize _____
Are you aware that _____
You may be surprised to learn that _____
Strangely enough, _____
Indeed, _____
Most people are unfamiliar with _____
Experience shows that _____
Most people agree that _____

TOPIC: The Ostrich
Main Idea #1: Appearance
Main Idea #2: Where They Live
Main Idea #3: Behavior

TOPIC: Skateboarding
Main Idea #1: Popular Sport
Main Idea #2: Equipment Needed
Main Idea #3: Safety Tips

TOPIC: The Space Shuttle
Main Idea #1: Appearance
Main Idea #2: Special Shuttle Missions
Main Idea #3: Future of Shuttle Travel

TOPIC: Connecticut
Main Idea #1: Beautiful Landscape
Main Idea #2: History
Main Idea #3: Tourist Attractions

TOPIC: Disney World
Main Idea #1: Key Attractions
Main Idea #2: Where to Stay
Main Idea #3: How to Get There

TOPIC: Feeding the Birds
Main Idea #1: Kinds of Feeders
Main Idea #2: Kinds of Birds You'll Attract
Main Idea #3: Kinds of Bird Seed

Activity:

Take a Second Look at Past Work

Another valuable activity involves looking back over pieces written earlier in the year and checking main-idea sentences for two reasons:

1. To determine if they are broad, yet distinct

2. To determine if they are varied and contain interesting language

My colleague Linda Chandler, a veteran fifth-grade teacher, got a lot of mileage out of this activity. Linda read over a set of papers her class had written on the topic, "What Do You Look for in a Friend?" Struck by the narrow range of main-idea sentences her students wrote, Linda went through the papers and typed out a representative sampling for use in a lesson:

> A good friend is wonderful to have.
> Friendship is always important to people.
> My friend always lets me do cool stuff with her.
> A friend is so awesome.
> Being with friends is great.
> Having a best friend is a good thing.
> A friend is fun to have.
> Friends are interesting.
> A good friend is someone who is nice.

Next, Linda made a transparency of this list and shared it with the whole class. The students, who at this point had been working on expository writing for a while, realized that the main-idea sentences were much too broad and indistinct. Through discussion and questioning, Linda helped them recognize how overly general adjectives serve to weaken a piece, rather than strengthen it. Students saw that words such as "wonderful," "nice," "awesome," "cool," "fun," and "great," carry little meaning. They also recognized that the sentence variety was poor, pointing out that almost all of the sentences began with some variation of "A friend . . ." or "My friend . . ." or "A good friend . . . ."

After the discussion, Linda conducted a Pick, List, and Choose lesson to help her students come up with a stronger prewriting plan. (See page 46.) Then, they used that plan, now made up of broad yet distinct main ideas, to construct concise, varied main-idea sentences. This was an engaging way to build on previous experience in a positive way.

When Main Ideas Don't Begin Paragraphs or Aren't Even Stated

As experienced adult readers, we recognize that main-idea sentences do not always come at the beginning of the paragraph. The details may build upon one another, and the main-idea sentence may tie them together at the end of the paragraph. For example:

> *Imagine seeing the Colosseum, the Piazza Navona, and the Pantheon. Lunch can be whatever you'd like—pasta at a small trattoria, panini at an outdoor cafe—even a Big Mac, for Americans who might be homesick! After a hardy lunch, it's on to the Sistine Chapel and Vatican Museums. No one ever leaves without a visit to the Spanish Steps and the Trevi Fountain. <u>Without a doubt, a walking tour of Rome is packed with adventure, history, and charm.</u>*

We also recognize that main ideas can be unstated, as in this paragraph, for example:

> *The mystery section of the bookstore often intrigues those curious by nature. The hopeless romantics head for the hundreds of romance novels. A wide selection of straight-ahead, no-nonsense nonfiction on thousands of topics often appeals to practical, detail-oriented individuals. An appealing children's section is stocked with picture books, beginning readers, middle-grade novels, and young adult fiction. Fans of poetry, short stories, biographies, and classic and contemporary literature will also not be disappointed by today's super-size bookstores.*

The implied main idea here is that today's super-sized bookstores have something for everyone.

While it is fairly easy to find published examples of the culminating main idea as well as the unstated main idea, I do not encourage inexperienced expository writers to try them. Imagine spending a month or more discussing the organization of an expository piece, conceptualizing broad yet distinct main ideas, finally writing paragraphs containing good word choice and sentence variety, and then telling students that it isn't necessary to begin their paragraphs with a main-idea sentence and that sometimes main-idea sentences are not even stated! Some students would ask, "Why include main-idea sentences at all?"

A main-idea sentence stated clearly at the beginning of each paragraph encourages the student to remain focused by backing up the idea with relevant details. That said, you still should be ready to discuss culminating and implied main ideas with your students, especially if you're asking them to read plenty of nonfiction through "author's eyes." When questions come up, I tell my students that, while authors do sometimes end their paragraphs with a main-idea sentence or by simply implying their main idea, less experienced writers would do better to state their main ideas at the beginning of paragraphs and move into more sophisticated techniques as they become comfortable with expository writing.

Activity:
Find the Missing Main Idea

To help students recognize and understand the concept of unstated main idea, I do an activity called "The Missing Main Idea." It not only is a great way to discuss unstated main ideas, but it gives students practice in identifying main-idea blurbs and translating them into effective sentences.

1. I explain to the class that I will hand out three paragraphs from the body of a piece of writing, with no introduction or conclusion. I also explain that I have left out each paragraph's main-idea sentence.

2. I divide the class into thirds and assign each group a paragraph to read thoroughly. Here are samples of paragraphs I might distribute. See reproducibles on pages 64 and 65.

> The mourning dove is a tawny buff colored bird with a blue ring around its dark eyes. During mating season you can notice the mourning dove's bright orange legs. These birds are the size of a common pigeon but have a sleeker, more attractive coat of feathers. Their wings are specked with black and they often have an iridescent appearance.
>
> The soft cooing call of the mourning dove is often heard before sunrise. Because of this some people mistakenly call this bird the "morning" dove. In fact they get their name from the sad, mournful cooing sound that they make. Their soothing call is sometimes mistaken for the hoot of an owl. Another sound that mourning doves make is a whistling sound caused by their wings moving during flight.

A small pile of sticks is all many doves require for a nest. Most doves are really very careless and sloppy nest builders. They often will prefer to take over the abandoned nest of some other bird, possibly adding a few twigs and leaves that they find nearby. These lazy nest builders sometimes simply lay eggs in between the branches of a tree without the benefit of any kind of nest at all!

3. I ask each group to decide what the paragraph is about and express it in a one-or two-word blurb in the margin. Then, together, we reconstruct the author's prewriting planner:

> TOPIC: Mourning doves
> Main Idea #1: Appearance
> Main Idea #2: Sounds they make
> Main Idea #3: Mourning dove nests

4. Finally, using the main-idea sentence starter chart, I ask students to translate their blurbs into a fluent, interesting main-idea sentence.

We might take a few minutes to brainstorm a number of word referents to use in place of the topic, mourning doves, for example "these interesting birds," "these fascinating creatures," "feathered friends," and so forth. Then, students construct main-idea sentences for each blurb, which we share. As a group, they come up with a wide variety of sentences and, in the process, recognize that they have many choices when it comes to constructing effective, interesting main-idea sentences.

This activity helps students understand an unstated main idea, while offering them practice in translating a basic prewriting plan into a series of main-idea sentences. On the next two pages, you'll find reproducible sets of paragraphs for your students to work with.

Name _____ Date _____

What's the Main Idea?: Mourning Doves

Directions: Each of these paragraphs is missing its main-idea sentence. Read each paragraph, decide what it's about, and then write an interesting main-idea sentence that makes sense.

1. The mourning dove is a tawny buff colored bird with a blue ring around its dark eyes. During mating season you can notice the mourning dove's bright orange legs. These birds are the size of a common pigeon but have a sleeker, more attractive coat of feathers. Their wings are specked with black and they often have an iridescent appearance.

_____

_____

2. The soft cooing call of the mourning dove is often heard before sunrise. Because of this some people mistakenly call this bird the "morning" dove. In fact they get their name from the sad, mournful cooing sound that they make. Their soothing call is sometimes mistaken for the hoot of an owl. Another sound that mourning doves make is a whistling sound caused by their wings moving during flight.

_____

_____

3. A small pile of sticks is all many doves require for a nest. Most doves are really very careless and sloppy nest builders. They often will prefer to take over the abandoned nest of some other bird, possibly adding a few twigs and leaves that they find nearby. These lazy nest builders sometimes simply lay eggs in between the branches of a tree without the benefit of any kind of nest at all!

_____

_____

Name _____ Date _____

What's the Main Idea?: Pumpkins

Directions: Each of these paragraphs is missing its main-idea sentence. Read each paragraph, decide what it's about, and then write an interesting main-idea sentence that makes sense.

1. Packets of pumpkin seeds can be bought in a garden center, hardware, or grocery store. Read the directions on the packet. Usually you plant the seeds in spring after the danger of frost is past. Make sure the soil is free of weeds and other plants. You can turn the soil over several times with a shovel and rake it through to soften it. Press your index finger into the soil to make a small hole about an inch and half deep. Simply place a seed in the hole, move over about eight inches and plant another seed there.

_____

_____

2. The pumpkin vines will spread in all directions throughout the spring and summer. Check them to make sure that insects aren't attacking the young plants. You may need to dust the plants with insect powder. The garden must be weeded and watered every few days. As tiny pumpkins form from the yellow blossoms you will want to check the undersides lying against the ground to prevent rot.

_____

_____

3. Full-grown pumpkins make beautiful fall decorations. People sit them on their front porches next to a group of corn stalks or a bale of hay. Halloween wouldn't be complete without a variety of jack-o-lanterns carved into scary grins. Of course, pumpkins are hollowed out for their pulp, which is seasoned and blended into spicy pumpkin pie filling. And don't forget the seeds—dry, salt, and roast some, and save the rest to plant next year!

_____

_____

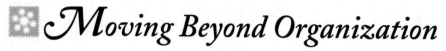 Moving Beyond Organization

Whether main ideas are clearly stated up front, unstated, or implied, they are the infrastructure of solidly constructed expository writing.

After guiding students through the exercises in the last two chapters, you will develop a base of skills that will help students as they craft expository pieces on their own.

The groundwork is laid, and now the fun part begins—working on elaboration, detail, and voice—the elements that transform the bare-bones infrastructure into a fully developed, attention-grabbing piece of writing.

At the moment, I am ready to finish off my seemingly never-ending kitchen renovation. The cabinets are in, hardwood floors are laid, counter tops in place, the walls and woodwork are freshly painted. It is clean, functional, and efficient. But what it lacks is a sense of the people who live and work in the space. In other words, I haven't yet added my own touches to it— the small richly detailed Oriental carpets, the antique green painted beveled mirror, my collection of green earthenware pottery and jadeware pitchers, the still-to-be determined simple window treatments, the green leafy fern that I imagine will hang from an antique brass hook above the sink. All these touches turn an efficient, highly functional space designed for the primary purpose of storing and preparing food into a comfortable space that reflects who I am as a person and that invites others in and encourages them to stay.

The same is true for expository writing. While the primary purpose is to organize information efficiently for the purpose of informing others, the skillful writer infuses something of herself or himself into it. In the following chapters we will plunge into supporting detail and voice, so that students can add their own finishing touches to their pieces.

Chapter 5

Identifying Supporting Details

What Makes Them Powerful?

I gather a group of fourth-grade students for a lesson. My objective is to engage them in a conversation that will help them see the importance of using details to support main ideas. As often happens, though, the conversation moves in a direction I don't anticipate but learn from nonetheless.

"I have something I want to share with you," I begin. "Some information I'd like you to have."

My students sit forward a little, waiting.

I take a deep breath and pause. "We've been studying the 50 states, and today we'll be talking about a state that is so beautiful it's been called 'The Land of Enchantment'—the state of New Mexico."

There is a murmuring through the group, some give and take about the states we've already studied and how their beauty might compare.

I pick up a piece of chalk, turn to the board, and write: "The landscape of New Mexico is enchanting."

"This is my main-idea sentence," I explain. "Now, as readers, what else do you want to know?"

The responses include, "What grows there?" "Are there mountains or plains?"

"Is it a desert?" "Are there hills?" and "What kind of climate?"

Laureen, who had made a diorama on the beautiful state of Wyoming, was not at all convinced that New Mexico could possibly be as enchanting as Wyoming. She narrowed her eyes. "How do we know that's true? That it's enchanting, I mean?"

There is a prove-it-to-me tone in her voice that throws me a little. This is not the direction in which I want to go. I pause and think about it. "How do we know that's true?" It's actually a terrific question. For sure, information needs to be convincing for the audience to accept and remember it.

"Good question, Laureen," I say. "Let's step away from New Mexico for a minute. If two of you come to me to report an incident on the bus, how do we sort out what actually happened—in other words, how do we get to what's true?"

Jimmy raises his hand and draws from one of his many run-ins on the bus: "You ask what happened, who saw what, who said what—and you try to get the story from a bunch of different kids."

The other children nod.

Danny adds, "If you get the same details from a bunch of kids, you know it's true. You know, like evidence and witnesses."

"Ah," I say. "Evidence. Witnesses. So what you're saying is that it isn't enough to tell me something like, 'Johnny was mean to me on the bus' and expect me to understand or believe it. If I'm to accept your argument, I'd need specific examples of what mean things he did, and I'd need it expressed in a number of ways. I'd also need to know why he behaved as he did. I'd need to know what caused him to act in a mean way and I'd also need to see how his behavior affected others."

The students nod.

I go to the chalkboard and write:

> CONVINCING DETAILS:
> Include a variety of specific examples.
> Show what you see, hear, smell, and feel.
> Explain cause and effect.
> Answer why the topic is important.

"We can apply these ideas to the Land of Enchantment, New Mexico. If I can give you specific examples of what makes the landscape beautiful (for example, the pinon tree, the cactus, the red rock, the turquoise sky, the ruby and amber sunsets), if I include details that involve the senses (for example, the warmth of the sun on the sandy earth, the prickly feel of the cactus, the sweet smell of desert flowers), and if I explain the way that centuries of harsh wind caused the rocks to wear into peculiar and amazing shapes, would you believe me?"

They all nod, even Laureen, although with a shrug.

Showing Information, Not Telling It

Have you ever been held captive by a museum guide—one who drones on, spewing fact after fact, date after date? The facts tend to slide off you because you have no images or experiences on which to hook them. All telling and no showing is not the best way to inform an audience. Once you get into the exhibit and begin to associate the facts and dates with awe-inspiring displays, the chances of holding onto the information increase.

The same is true for expository writing. The inexperienced writer will often simply state facts (i.e. telling), without offering examples, anecdotes, and interesting details (i.e. showing).

For example, here is a paragraph from Edward's paper on redecorating his room:

> I need more things in my room.
> I would like to have big fish tan
> in my room with goldfish in it. Another thing
> is a green and comfortable, inflatible
> sofa. One other thing I want in my
> room is an electric train that will
> go around my room.

Notice the way he *tells* each fact. He never shows us the information he wants us to absorb. He doesn't give us a clear sense of what this new-and-improved room will be like. As such, it is difficult for the reader to create a mental picture of the room. Edward doesn't explain why these things are important to him. And he could use some help with sentence variety.

For years I would have simply asked students go back and add details. But they had no idea exactly what I was looking for. They would insert color, size, and sometimes adjectives such as "terrific," "neat," "nice," "pretty," "great," or "awesome." For example, this was Edward's revision, with the details he added in boldface:

> I need more things in my room. I would like to have a big **glass** fish tank in my room with beautiful gold fish in it. Another thing is an **awesome** green and inflatable sofa. One other thing I want in my room is an **expensive** electric train that will go around my **cool** room.

The revision, as you can see, is not all that much better than the original. The adjectives don't add meaning. So my challenge became getting students to add relevant details that show rather than tell about the main idea they support. What kinds of details illustrate, explain, and/or convince the audience? What were the questions I needed to ask to help my students generate powerful supporting details?

Ask Detail-Generating Questions

Generating powerful details starts with asking the right questions. As authors work, they ask themselves questions that reveal information about their topic. The answers help them show, rather than tell, the reader about that topic.

In my years of working with students, I've come up with a list of questions that seem to work, regardless of what they're writing about. These questions not only help students elaborate on details but also encourage them to use good sentence variety.

The Questions

Have students read each paragraph in their piece and ask themselves:

What does each detail "look" like?

Encourage them to include not only what they see but also what they hear, feel, and smell.

This question motivates students to use vivid description by applying the five senses.

Why is this detail important?

This question reminds students to explain how each detail relates to the main idea. Answering it provides the reasons the writer included the detail in the first place.

Is each detail in a separate sentence?

This question is important for two reasons. It prevents the "grocery list" of details. And, if students have already created a grocery list, it forces them to prioritize their ideas and stick only to those that are most relevant. For example, if a student has to revise the following sentence into a series of sentences, with one detail in each, what do you think will happen?

"They sell Milky Ways, Kit Kats, Three Musketeers, Hershey Bars, Junior Mints, jelly beans, Reeses Peanut Butter Cups, Snowcaps, Raisinettes, and Good and Plenty."

Most likely, the student will look at the sentence closely and narrow the details down to a handful of important ones to illustrate his or her point.

Did I use specific examples to describe each detail?

Encourage them to stay away from phrases such as, "cool stuff," "awesome things," ". . . all kinds of," and ". . . and much more."

This question guides students toward spotting vague, worthless language and substituting it with something more precise. For example, "We did all kinds of fun stuff at camp" might lead to, "We hiked in the Smoky Mountains. Learning crafts with leather and tile was fun, too. Most people really enjoyed boating and archery."

Name _____ Date _____

Questions for Creating Powerful Details

Directions: Read over your draft and ask yourself the following questions to bring details to life.

What does each detail "look" like?

Include not only what you see but also what you hear, feel, and smell. Apply the five senses.

Why is each detail important?

How does it relate to the main idea? Why did you include it in the first place?

Is each detail in a separate sentence?

Try not to create a "grocery list" of details. If you already have created a grocery list, prioritize your ideas and keep only the most interesting and meaningful ones.

Did I use specific examples to describe each detail?

Stay away from phrases such as, "cool stuff," "awesome things," ". . . all kinds of," and ". . . and much more."

The Ford Truck Piece: What Detail-Generating Questions Look Like in Action

Here is a paragraph with a main-idea sentence that is supported by simply stated facts, rather than by details generated through the above questions:

> The Classic 1956 Ford F100 pick-up truck is stylish and practical. It has smooth lines and classic '50s detailing. The cab is roomy, with recovered seats, a new tape deck, original radio, large rear view mirror, and added seatbelts. The bed is large and lined with solid wood. It has a V-8 engine which has been rebuilt. Its sturdy body construction has lasted almost 50 years. It has a small steel steering wheel, large dice hanging from the rear view mirror, and many more cool features.

It tells and hardly shows. Watch how detail-generating questions serve to nudge the writer's thinking.

> The Classic 1956 Ford F100 pick-up truck is stylish and practical. It has smooth lines and classic '50s detailing. **(What does it look like?)** The cab is roomy, with recovered seats, a new tape deck, original radio, large rear view mirror, and added seatbelts. **(Is each detail in a separate sentence? Why is all of this important?)** The bed is large and lined with solid wood. **(Why is this important?)** It has a V-8 engine which has been rebuilt and its sturdy body construction has lasted almost 50 years. **(Is each detail in a separate sentence? Why is all of this important?)** It has a small steel steering wheel, large dice hanging from the rear view mirror, and many more cool features. **(Can you give a specific example of that?)**

Here's the revision, the original paragraph enhanced by answers to the detail-generating questions:

> The Classic 1956 Ford F100 pick-up truck is stylish and practical. It has smooth lines and classic 50s detailing. Large, curved fenders cover the wheels. The headlights are round, with shiny metal trim. The F100 model name is highlighted in a chevron pattern of chrome which runs along the edge of the hood. The cab is roomy, large enough for three good-sized adult passengers. The seats have been recovered in an attractive, yet durable blue nylon fabric. A new tape deck has been installed which augments the original 1950s radio. An extra-wide rear view mirror provides a clear view out the back of the cab window. For safety reasons, seatbelts have been added. The truck bed is large and lined with solid wood—perfect for hauling furniture or gardening equipment. The wood also resists rust, which is a real problem in many older vehicles. The rebuilt V-8 engine uses unleaded gas, and is easy to repair and

maintain. Its sturdy body construction has lasted almost 50 years, which proves that it has been well cared for. The small steel steering wheel comes equipped with a half-circular horn. An oversized plush set of red dice hangs from the rear view mirror. Wooden running boards grace the sides of the cab for easy entry.

Create "Wow" Pieces with a Paragraph Make-Over

To help students use these questions to best advantage, I model how to use them in a piece of writing. Usually, I share a before-and-after example that I've done, such as the Ford truck paragraph. Then I ask students to volunteer one of their paragraphs for a "make-over."

1. I begin by stressing how we can take a satisfactory piece of writing and transform it into a "wow" piece. When I ask students for a piece to work with, I usually get a flurry of raised hands and a chorus of "Ooh, Oohs!" Just about everyone wants to be "made-over."

2. I choose a piece that has good organization but minimal elaboration. I make a transparency of the piece and place it on the overhead. As we read and analyze the piece together, I look for and point out the strong points, as well as the opportunities for elaboration. (When I refer to minimal elaboration as an opportunity, rather than a weakness, students are more eager to participate in the revision process. Having opportunities is positive. Having weaknesses isn't.)

3. I ask the questions related to the facts, encouraging the entire class to give me detailed answers. I translate their responses into revisions that I write on the piece, using overhead markers.

Here is an example of a revision we completed as a class. I've included the three versions: the original, the original with my questions inserted, and the final revision.

Mill River (Original Piece)

Do you enjoy nature as much as I do? If so, Mill River is the best place to go to enjoy nature. I will tell you about the nature and wildlife of Mill River.

I bet you couldn't imagine the sights of the beautiful birds at Mill River. Usually you'll see kingfishers, ducks, or cormorants, maybe even some herons. You could also see snowy egrets, geese, and robins. Two of the prettiest sights I saw there were two robins on the lawn of the Red Mill House and the goose laying eggs on a little island in the middle of the river.

You shouldn't miss out on seeing the animals at Mill River. You would probably see a muskrat near a swamp or a tree. You also might see a snake in a bush like the one I saw at Cobble Island. You might see a skunk at night somewhere near Mill River. If you don't like squirrels, don't go to Mill River—there are lots of squirrels there.

If you're a plant and tree kind of person stop at Mill River, there are so many kinds of trees and plants there. One common tree is the maple, which has some sap on it and has leaves that look like the Canadian flag. Another kind of tree is the sycamore which has a trunk that looks camouflaged. One kind of plant that is there is the trout lily whose blossom looks like the trout fish. You will see these and many other kinds of plants.

Well, if you like birds, animals, or plants and trees, you're definitely a Mill River kind of person. The best times to visit are spring and summer. So, get your binoculars, camera, and hiking shoes and head to Mill River!

Although the student has included quite a bit of information, the piece has a "listy" quality. Also note the lack of sentence variety: "You would see, You probably would see, You also might see . . ." "One kind of tree, Another kind of tree . . ." "One kind of plant, Another kind of plant . . ." and so forth. These are the areas I will zero in on. Since, at this point in time, we haven't worked on introductions and conclusions, I will leave those sections alone.

Mill River (Original Piece with Detail-Generating Questions Added)

I write in these questions as we read through the piece, then go back and address them one by one on a separate transparency or on chart paper. I write in student suggestions. I also underline redundant sentence structure and brainstorm better ways to begin these sentences.

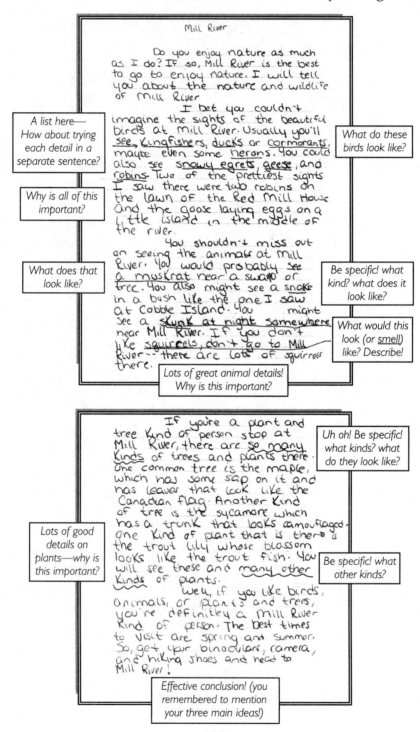

Here is the class revision:

Mill River (Final Revision)

Do you enjoy nature as much as I do? If so, Mill River is the best place to go to enjoy nature. I will tell you about the nature and wildlife of Mill River.

I bet you couldn't imagine the sights of the beautiful birds at Mill River. Usually you'll see pointy beaked kingfishers along the riverbank. Brown and green mallard ducks can be seen paddling by. Cormorants dip and dive beneath the water hunting for food. You might even spot some graceful herons wading in the shallow water. Long necked snowy egrets are common sights near the riverbanks. Canadian geese live here year round, while robins appear in the spring. Two of the prettiest sights I saw there were two red-breasted robins on the lawn of the Red Mill House and the patient goose nesting, laying eggs on a little island in the middle of the river. Clearly, Mill River is an important habitat for a wide variety of birds.

You shouldn't miss out on seeing the animals at Mill River. On most days the patient observer can spy a sleek brown muskrat near a swamp or a tree. A small tan garter snake like the one I saw at Cobble Island can be spotted sunning itself in a bush. You might not actually see a skunk at night somewhere near Mill River but you certainly might smell one! If you don't like frisky gray squirrels, don't go to Mill River—there are lots of squirrels there. Mill River is a sanctuary for these small woodland creatures and a wonderful place for animal lovers to observe and appreciate them.

If you're a plant and tree kind of person, stop at Mill River. There are so many kinds of trees and plants there. One common tree is the maple, which has some sticky amber colored sap on it and has leaves that look like the Canadian flag. The sycamore tree is interesting because its speckled, peeling trunk looks camouflaged. Growing nearby are the trout lilies whose long, tapered blossoms look like the trout fish. Of course there are other varieties of native plants, such as the rhododendron with its long, narrow green leaves and large pink and white blossoms and the Connecticut State plant, the mountain laurel, with its small bell-shaped flowers. This large variety of trees, plants, and bushes provides shelter and food for the birds and animals that live there.

Well, if you like birds, animals, or plants and trees, you're definitely a Mill River kind of person. The best times to visit are spring and summer. So, get your binoculars, camera, and hiking shoes and head to Mill River!

It is helpful to model many revisions with students so that they begin to anticipate and internalize the detail-generating questions. I also keep a large chart with these questions hanging at all times, to remind students to question as they write. In time, they will apply them automatically in their own work.

For more reluctant students, pinpoint a single sentence that needs revision. Once you finish, choose another sentence or two. Breaking down revision one step at a time makes the task less overwhelming.

- •What does it look like? (DESCRIBE!)
- •Why is it important?
- •Did you give a specific example?
  (AVOID: stuff, all kinds of, every type of, and much more!!)
- •Is each detail in a separate sentence?
  (AVOID THE GROCERY LIST!)

Asking questions like these strengthens details.

Activity:

Enhance Sentence Variety by Moving the Subject

Here is a revision tip that helps with sentence variety: Move the subject. Here's what I mean. Suppose a student writes the following paragraph:

> Grizzly bears are magnificent to look at. They have dark shaggy fur. They have sharp claws and teeth. They have long snouts. They have very small tails. They stand over six feet tall.

Now read the revision:

> Grizzly bears are magnificent to look at. Dark shaggy fur covers their bodies. Sharp claws and teeth allow them to catch and kill their prey. Their long snouts help them sniff out food and smell danger. A very small tail may flick this way and that when they are frightened, angry, or excited. Standing upright, grizzly bears often top six feet!

The subject of each detail sentence (i.e. "they") has been shifted or changed to add more variety and, therefore, interest. After modeling this kind of revision for students, let students try their hand at it, using the following examples, one at a time:

There is a velvet couch against the wall.
There is a wool Oriental carpet on the floor.
There are silk curtains on the windows.
There are large windows in the front of the room.
There is a marble topped table in the corner.
There is an old oak desk in the middle of the room.

Encourage students to use active verbs and then string the sentences together into a paragraph. Compare the before-and-after versions. Be sure to discourage students from constructing all the sentences the same way, since the point is to vary the sentence structure within the paragraph.

> There is a velvet couch against the wall. or . . . .
> Against the wall stands a velvet couch.
>
> There are silk curtains on the window. or . . . .
> The windows are graced with silk curtains.
>
> There is a wool Oriental carpet on the floor. or . . . .
> The floor is covered with a wool Oriental carpet.

Between the use of the detail-generating questions and opportunities for varying sentence structure, students' writing will begin to become more fully and fluently elaborated. It will begin to show rather than simply tell.

Making Our Writing Our Own

I end this chapter with a paragraph "make-over" topic—my kitchen, a work-in-progress. In the first paragraph I'll *tell* you about the progress. In the second, I'll *show* you.

> The kitchen is about 90 percent completed. The cabinets are in and stocked. The butcher block counter tops have been installed and finished. The hardwood floor was just sanded, stained, and sealed. Some decorations have been hung on the walls and favorite kitchen items have been placed here and there.

Can you picture my kitchen? Probably not. Aren't you wondering what it looks like? Why butcher block is important? What some of my favorite items are? Now, read the revision:

> The kitchen is about 90 percent completed. The almond hued cabinets dressed with crystal knobs and Victorian brass drawer pulls are in and fully stocked. The deep drawers and wide cabinets with roll-out shelves provide a convenient place for dishes, utensils, cookware, and canned and dry goods. There is a place within easy reach for just about everything. The butcher block counter tops, stained to a medium golden brown, project a cozy glow, warming the space and complementing the expanse of pale cabinetry. Sanding, staining, and sealing the oak hardwood floors was a messy job but well worth it. The effect is purely country, while being resilient and requiring little care. Scroll-shaped brass brackets top the windows, which await lush green hanging plants.

A grapevine wreath displays depression-era red and green kitchen gadgets tied in place with calico ribbons.

So, does that give you a better sense of the state of my kitchen? What it still needs are powerful details—the kind that will make my kitchen mine and only mine. Right now it's lovely, but it looks a little like something out of a catalog. In the final go-round I'll be finessing it, searching for the kinds of accessories, antiques, and collectibles that will clearly define who I am.

Likewise, in the next chapter we will examine strategies for writing a variety of extremely powerful supporting details that can make a good piece of writing truly one's own.

Chapter 6

Writing Powerful Supporting Details

I walk into the local junk shop and, amidst the STP Oil sign, raccoon coat, and lobster-trap coffee table, I see it—the object that will transform my kitchen from a lovely but generic room into one uniquely mine. It's a rectangular, beveled mirror in a green milk-painted frame, topped with a carved, fan-shaped medallion. It's large, probably 36-by-24 inches. The glass is smoky, a sign of its age, and, I believe, an indication that it's seen and taken in a lot. I imagine it gracing a length of wall, expanding and "cozying up" the kitchen all at once. I write out the check without haggling over the price, drag the mirror home, and nag my husband to hang it immediately.

I gaze into my purchase and smile. It brings the whole room together, just as I thought it would, because it tells—or rather shows—a little something about who I am. I'm amazed at how the right detail can have such a powerful impact.

Writers also use the right details to dress up paragraphs, to illustrate main ideas in memorable ways, and to bring their writing to life. And "reading with an author's eyes" is a good way to discover the kinds of techniques professional writers use. Try rereading a magazine article that you found particularly interesting and informative. What details jump out at you? What do you take away from the article as memorable and thought provoking? Here are some excerpts that jumped out at me recently:

Fishguts, walnuts, and tomatoes. What do these three items have in common? They were some of the original ingredients used to make that popular condiment, ketchup.
—*Boys' Quest*, August/September, 1999

Look at a basic eight stud LEGO brick. If you have six of these, you can combine them in 102,981,500 different ways. In other words, LEGO collectors have millions of choices.
—*Boys' Quest*, August/September, 1999

Early mariners were said to seek refuge in the little harbor that was "snug as a booth." Today visitors from around the world come to share the breathtaking beauty and adventure of the region's rocky coastline reaching into the sea; the tranquility of woodland trails scented with pine, cedar, and salt air; and the charm of coastal life.
—*Official 1999 Guidebook of the Boothbay Harbor Region*

Imagine being hauled up hundreds of feet in the air, flung down toward the ground at speeds nearing 100 miles per hour, yanked upward so hard you feel you're being crushed, then flipped upside down and swung side to side until you're about to lose your lunch.
—*Muse*, July/August, 2000

In addition to their many direct service programs Actors and Others is a strong advocate for the welfare of animals. The organization supports legislation, which protects animals and works to abolish needless suffering through passing of new laws. "We never give up on an animal," said M.A.S.H. star Loretta Swit.
—*Pet Life*, July/August, 1999

Supporting Main Ideas with "Golden Bricks"

My grade partner, Dea Auray, and I realized that excerpts like these were too good to keep from our students. So we began collecting, analyzing, and categorizing these little nuggets of specificity to create a menu of examples for students to draw from. We scanned all the high-quality children's and adult magazines we could find.

We referred to those nuggets as "Golden Bricks" because of the brick-like detail boxes in the expository pillar described on page 24. We thought that if each detail was a brick, and students needed at least four bricks to support each main idea, at least one of those bricks should be exceptionally powerful. Hence, the term Golden Bricks. We assumed that each paragraph would dramatically improve if our students added at least one Golden Brick to illustrate the main idea. The Golden Bricks we found authors using fell into these categories:

♦ quotes   ♦ statistics

♦ amazing facts   ♦ anecdotes

♦ descriptive segments

Lesson:

Make Details More Memorable with "Golden Bricks"

Here is a whole-class lesson that I use for introducing students to the Golden Bricks.

1. I begin by choosing a topic they are familiar with, such as the first day of school, and jot down a simple prewriting plan on a chart:

TOPIC: The First Day of School
Main Idea #1: A New Teacher
Main Idea #2: Supplies You'll Need
Main Idea #3: Making New Friends

2. I explain that we will be concentrating on main idea #2: Supplies You'll Need. On the overhead, I show the following paragraph:

There are a number of school supplies to have on hand for the first day of school. Of course, two or three bright yellow, sharpened, #2 pencils are important. Another essential is a sturdy three ring binder with lined paper for taking notes. Most teachers insist that you have a box for keeping track of your pencils, crayons, and markers. Finally, a large, comfortable backpack is necessary for carrying all of your books and supplies back and forth to school.

"*The Golden Bricks*"

Directions: Here are five ways to liven details in your expository pieces. As you write and revise, use this list for inspiration.

A Quote The words of an authority on the subject being addressed. Be sure to tell the reader who the expert is and what his/her qualifications are.
Example: "Miss Patricia Stosak, veteran sixth-grade teacher says, 'Sixth graders are the most lively, social, talkative, and spirited people I know.'"

A Statistic Information presented as a number, ratio, or percentage.
Examples: "On average, 200 people visit this web site daily." "Nearly seven out of 10 people who visit the web site order one of our products." "Ninety-nine percent of our customers reorder online."

An Amazing Fact An unusual fact that will surprise readers.
Example: "The blue-gray gnatcatcher (a small Northeastern bird) actually holds its elegant nest together with spider silk, then covers it with lichens for camouflage!"

An Anecdote A short, explicit story used to illustrate a main idea.
Example: "That reminds me of the time I wore my clogs and slipped on the icy path. This is just another example of why it is important to dress appropriately for the weather."

A Descriptive Segment A vivid two or three sentence description that uses the five senses to illustrate an example.
Example: "Cars and buses rush past in a blur. Taxi horns blare. The air is filled with the smell of exhaust. Pedestrians crowd the sidewalks. Skyscrapers tower over-head. The city is a bustling place!"

"Okay," I begin. "This is a pretty strong paragraph."

The kids nod as they reread the piece.

3. We look at the piece, sentence by sentence. "Read the first sentence silently," I say. "Did the author ask and answer our detail-generating questions: What does it look like and why is it important?"

Their lips move silently, eyes narrow, and a sea of hands appear.

"Shannon?"

Shannon points to the paragraph. "The author tells what it looks like—the pencil—but not why it's important."

"Good. Who can revise it?"

Nicholas calls out, "Just add on to that pencil sentence . . . for written work and for taking down assignments."

The others nod.

"Great," I say. "That way we've included not only what it looks like but why it's important." I add a caret and write in his revision. "How about the next sentence . . . the one about the notebook?"

"Hmmm . . ." Gregory mumbles. "It's okay. The author describes it and explains what you use it for. But, you can still spruce it up a little . . ."

I raise an eyebrow. "Shoot," I say. Other hands wave.

Gregory accepts the challenge. "Another essential is a sturdy three ring binder with plastic pockets for important papers. Fill it with lined paper *with reinforced holes* so you won't lose your work."

"Much better!" I say as I write in his revision, "Great word choice!"

We go on in similar fashion to the next detail about the supply box. Finally we come to the last detail, the backpack, and I pause. "You know, a Golden Brick would really add something to this paragraph, maybe a statistic or a quote about the backpack." I wait, letting that idea sink in.

"Let's go with a quote," I decide. "What authority can you come up with on the subject of being prepared for school? Someone who has told you something about the importance of a backpack?"

There is a buzz of conversation. Students share responses such as, "my mother", "Mrs. Mariconda", "the principal", "our school bus driver."

"Let's see," I begin. "Whose mother has had something to say about a backpack?" Based on the show of hands, everyone's mother is a quotable expert.

"Emily?" I ask. "What does your mother have to say about a backpack?"

Emily smiles and reports, "My mother says that a backpack is the best way to get your homework back and forth in one piece."

"Excellent," I say. "But you didn't state it as a direct quote. You paraphrased what your mom said. Here's how we write that as a direct quote. First we identify the expert." I write:

> Mrs. Harrison, mother of three school-age children, says . . .

"Next I add quotation marks around our expert's words." I complete the sentence:

> Mrs. Harrison, mother of three school-age children, says, "Using a backpack is the best way to get your homework back and forth in one piece."

"See how the quote adds power to the paragraph?" I ask.

The children nod.

I go on. "Now it's your turn. Choose an expert and write your own quote about the value of a backpack."

4. As students work, I circulate around the room, reminding them to use the quotation marks and to identify their expert. They do an excellent job and, together, we finish the revision:

> There are a number of school supplies to have on hand for the first day of school. Of course, two or three bright yellow, sharpened, #2 pencils are important for written work and for taking down assignments. Another essential is a sturdy three ring binder with plastic pockets for important papers. Fill it with lined paper with reinforced holes so you won't lose your work. Most teachers insist that you have a clear plastic box for keeping track of your pencils, crayons, and markers. Finally, a large, comfortable backpack is necessary for carrying all of your books and supplies. Mrs. Harrison, mother of three school age children says, "Using a backpack is the best way to get your homework back and forth to school in one piece."

I use this procedure for each type of Golden Brick. Notice that some of these Golden Bricks require research. If you were writing about the characteristics of the great horned owl, for example, you probably wouldn't know, off the top of your head, what an ornithologist might say. You probably would not have any statistics at your fingertips regarding this creature, nor an amazing fact. You might have an anecdote about a time you saw a great horned owl and, based on former knowledge, use it in your piece, but that might not be the best way to support your main idea.

Although it is never ethical to "make up" a quote, statistic, or amazing fact and publish it as fact, I make an exception to this rule when we are practicing the writing skill. For the purpose of practice, I might allow the class to "create" an expert quote or statistic, since my objective is to provide an opportunity for students to try out the strategy.

For example, if our main idea was that cotton candy is a popular carnival treat, we might create the following Golden Brick: "Stan Smith, long time carnival concession worker, says, 'I sell more cotton candy than anything else!'" I then explain to students that, if they wanted to actually use a quote like this in a published piece, they would need to research it—call or visit a real concession worker, for example.

Similarly, we might create a statistic for practice purposes, so that I can see if my students understand how to use and express it properly. For example, to support my students' impression that most kids prefer pizza over other school lunches, we might claim: "As many as 90 percent of students polled agree that pizza is their favorite school cafeteria food choice." They could use that statistic as a placeholder in their draft, but I would require them to do research, possibly by polling their lunch shift, to verify or modify it for accuracy. This makes an excellent math activity—gathering data and expressing results as a percentage, a ratio, a pie chart, or bar graph.

Extending the "Golden Bricks" Lesson by Exploring One Detail in Multiple Ways

To reinforce ideas, try expressing one detail in different ways, by applying each of the Golden Bricks to it: quote, statistic, amazing fact, anecdote, and descriptive segment. Devote one lesson to each brick. I'll show you what I mean using the backpack detail: "A backpack is an essential school supply."

1. In lesson one, I model using a quote by asking, "What expert might have something to say about a backpack?" I write the example, "Fifth-grade teacher Linda Chandler always says, 'Lugging your books home from school in your arms is a lot more difficult than carrying them in a comfortable, well-constructed backpack!'" I also point out that the expert is named and identified.

2. In lesson two, I model using a statistic by asking, "What do a majority of people think about backpacks?" I write the example, "In fact, 95 percent of Mill Hill fifth graders polled say they spent more money on the perfect backpack than on any other school supply." I also point out that the way this statistic is stated reveals how the information was acquired.

3. In lesson three, I model using an amazing fact by asking, "What truly surprises you about a backpack?" I write the example, "Have you ever stopped to realize that backpacks are perhaps the only school supply item used by students in kindergarten all the way through

1. **Define and Discuss Golden Bricks** Begin by sharing examples of each type of Golden Brick. You can use the ones on the previous page or find your own.

2. **Find Published Examples** Have students search through magazines and clip examples of paragraphs containing a Golden Brick. Make a chart for each category: Quote, Statistic, Amazing Fact, Anecdote, and Descriptive Segment. Glue clippings on the appropriate charts and share them with the class. This also makes a terrific ongoing homework assignment.

3. **Model** Take a paragraph that contains mostly simply stated facts and ask students how one of the Golden Bricks might help illustrate the main idea. (See the sample lesson on page 87.)

4. **Provide Guided Practice** Encourage students to revise that paragraph by applying the same type of Golden Brick in a different way. Circulate and offer encouragement, guidance, and constructive criticism. Share effective revisions with the class. On subsequent days, encourage students to try other types of Golden Bricks.

5. **Promote Application** During writers' workshop, have students apply the technique to a piece they are working on. This might involve some research to locate sources for quotes, statistics, and amazing facts. Your media specialist may be an excellent resource.

graduate school?" I also point out that asking a question is just one way to express an amazing fact.

4. In lesson four, I model using an anecdote by asking, "Can you describe a time when you found a backpack helpful or a time when you wished you had had one?" I write the example, "I'll never forget the time I left my backpack home and had to carry three books, my notebook, lunch bag, diorama, and my homework folder home. I dropped everything on the bus and watched my things slide all over the dirty floor. After that, I made sure I always had my backpack!" I also point out that the last sentence connects back to the idea that backpacks are necessary.

5. In lesson five, I model using a descriptive segment by asking, "What would the perfect backpack look and feel like?" I write the example, "Backpacks crafted of soil-resistant canvas in navy blue, forest green, or black are especially popular. For the best storage, at least three roomy, zippered compartments are a must. The straps should be wide and heavily cushioned so that they rest comfortably on your shoulders, even when holding ten pounds of textbooks!" I also point out that this description is not a grocery list: "Your backpack could be navy blue, forest green, or black, soil resistant, roomy with zippered compartments, and wide cushioned straps." And it is not a broken record either: "It should be canvas. It should be soil resistant. It should be navy blue, forest green, or black."

Applying each Golden Brick to the same detail demonstrates to students that authors have many ways to present information.

Activity:

Share Sentence Starters

Typically, students learn quickly how to recognize Golden Bricks. The challenge, I've found, is getting students to use them effectively and fluently in their own writing. One way to help is by creating sentence-starter charts, one for each kind of brick, which students can refer to as they write. Your charts might look like this:

Quote

_____ says, "_____ ."
      Name/title

Just ask _____ who says, "_____ ."
              Name/title

Experts such as _____ agree. She/He says, "_____ ."
             Name/title

Statistic

You might be surprised to learn that _____ .

In fact, _____ .

Statistics show that _____ .

Most people don't realize that _____ .

Amazing Fact

Amazingly, _____ .

Most people are shocked to realize that _____ .

It is surprising, but _____ .

Incredibly, _____ .

Anecdote

I'll never forget the time when _____ .
An illustration of this was when _____ .
I will always remember the time when _____ .
For example, _____ .

Descriptive Segment

Have you ever seen _____ ?
Take a good look at _____ .
Let's examine the _____ .
Would you recognize _____ ?

Be sure to add examples to each chart over time, as you encounter them in books, magazines, and your students' own work. Point out that not every sentence starter will work with every topic—that, as authors, students need to "try out" a number of different bricks and sentence starters before they find the best ones. The point is, students need to have a number of options, a bank of choices.

Extending the "Golden Brick" Lesson with Projects

Another terrific "Golden Brick" extension activity involves art and special projects. Writing is often difficult to manage because some students finish much more quickly than others. I always found myself trying to slow some students down while prodding others to work more quickly. Having a related art or research project allows students the time they need to write and experiences to keep them tuned in once they're satisfied with the writing they've done. As such, I use these projects as enrichment and a tool for time management. Here are some projects that extend expository writing:

♦ Collect related Golden Bricks through a variety of research resources—books, magazines, videos, the Internet, interviews.

♦ Create a class mural of a setting they are writing about (rain forest, tundra, woodland, seashore, marshland, prairie, desert).

♦ Create a pie chart, bar graph, or line graph showing statistics on a topic. (There are many computer programs that will translate raw data into these kinds of visual tools.)

♦ Draw or paint a detailed, labeled diagram of an object related to the topic.

♦ Draw a portrait of a person, a landscape of a setting, or a still life of an object that they are writing about.

Consider Small, Flexible Groups to Reach Every Student

In every classroom, in every grade, there is a wide range of students at vastly different places in their development as writers. Some students begin the year writing stream-of-consciousness, disorganized expository pieces. Your short-term objective for them, most likely, is recognition and mastery of basic organization. From there, you can move to creating broad yet distinct main ideas and asking simple detail-generating questions such as what it looks like or why it's important.

Others in your class may have already mastered basic organization and are ready to move on to studying main ideas and supporting details. And, if you are like most teachers, you have a couple of natural writers who soak up and apply your instruction.

So how do you meet the needs of all students without holding some back and pushing others beyond their abilities? You might choose to introduce the Golden Brick strategy to a smaller, flexible group of students, rather than to the entire class. You can send the group to the media center with some specific research goals (for example, to find a quote from Abe Lincoln, a statistic about Arizona's natural resources, an amazing fact about the starfish), while you work more closely with students who have not yet mastered planning a piece, coming up with main ideas, or crafting supporting details. Reconfigure the research group periodically, adding or removing students as their needs change and skills improve.

♦ Construct a diorama that illustrates a topic.

♦ Make a collage on a given topic.

♦ Make a map with a key that gives information about a place they are writing about.

♦ Collect a variety of books on their topic and make a bibliography.

♦ Create a timeline with small illustrations to indicate historical changes.

How can these projects be used to the best advantage in the classroom? Translating information helps students look at their topic in new ways, which enhances their writing. For students whose thinking is too concrete, many of these projects will inspire ideas and open up possibilities.

What I like best about these projects, though, is using them as a means for managing writers' workshop. If I give an assignment (for example, to write an expository piece about a woodland creature we've studied), I'll have some students who can immediately and independently lay out a simple prewriting plan, begin constructing main-idea sentences, and go on to write a decent piece. I'll have others who need review and reinforcement of the skills I've taught. Before I give the assignment, I assess where my students are and divide them into three flexible groups. (I never refer to groups as groups, by the way. I simply call together the students by name, "John, Cindy, Sara, William . . .") The groups consist of:

1. Those who can proceed with planning and writing independently

2. Those who need a small amount of review and some direction to get started

3. Those who need a lot of direction and guidance to write

Next, I introduce the assignment, as well as the related projects, to the whole class. For example, I'd explain that everyone will write an expository piece about a woodland creature, will contribute to a class mural of the woodland habitat, and will create a crayon and watercolor wash of their creature of choice, which will eventually be bound, along with their expository piece, into a class "Woodland Field Guide." I am confident that everyone in the class will be excited by some aspect of this project.

I ask members of group #1 to come up with a simple prewriting plan: the topic and at least three main-idea blurbs. I'll check their plans before they go on.

I invite members of group #2 to decide on their creature, get a large piece of construction paper, and begin to sketch that creature. I make a number of books available for reference. As they look at the books, they store away information to include later in their writing.

Since members of group #3 need the most direction, I lead them through the Pick, List, and Choose procedure described on page 46 and assist them in choosing their own creature and identifying three broad yet distinct main ideas. I might work with each member, one on one. As they wait for me, or as they finish, they move to the mural, as do members of group #1.

On subsequent days, I might send group #1 members to the media center to find examples of Golden Bricks, while I walk group #2 members through their prewriting plans. Group #3 members take their next small step toward writing independently. I might move some students to other groups, based on their progress and interest level. Eventually, everyone has worked on the mural, completed their watercolor wash based on their creature, and written their expository piece.

From the Work's Body to Its "Bookends"

Too often, students view expository writing as straightforward, dry, and not nearly as creative as narrative writing. But as they begin to see the many options they have—showing rather than telling, using detail-generating questions and Golden Bricks, extending their writing through projects—they begin to realize that writing expository pieces does not have to be boring. These options allow them to deliver information with creativity, variety, and style.

Once students begin applying these options, the hardest work is done. The body of their piece is solid. So I turn to "the bookends"—the beginning and ending, which flank the body and hold it together.

Chapter 7

Crafting Introductions

Making a Good First Impression

To use my back door, you must pass through a real eyesore—an unfinished laundry room. The walls are sheetrock, the floors plywood. There is no woodwork yet, no paint on the walls. There is nothing inviting about this small utilitarian space that my family and I pass through every time we enter the house. True, after a few steps we're rewarded with finding ourselves in our kitchen, but I often wonder what kind of impression the entrance makes on first-time guests.

My laundry room reminds me of many of my students' introduction paragraphs. Once you get past them, things improve. Their pieces' bodies are usually good. But first impressions count. In some ways, an introduction paragraph is the most important part of a piece; if it's boring, after all, the reader will not be inclined to read on. Case in point:

> This report will give you information about flight. I will tell you how ancient people dreamed of flying, about the invention of the airplane, and about today's space shuttle.

Clearly, we know what the piece of writing will be about and the author's purpose. In fact, we can reduce the introduction to a prewriting plan pretty easily:

TOPIC: Flight
Main Idea #1: Ancient Desire to Fly
Main Idea #2: Invention of the Plane
Main Idea #3: The Space Shuttle

The author has a solid plan, but after reading the introduction, do you care? The writer seems as bored as I am. Compare that introduction to this one:

> Take a moment to consider Icarus and his melting wings; Leonardo Da Vinci's inspiring, yet unsuccessful, flying machine; and our own generation's contribution to flight, the Space Shuttle. Throughout the ages, human beings have yearned to soar above the clouds. Exploring the history of flight, which includes the dreams of the ancients, the invention of the airplane, and the use of today's space shuttle, is an amazing journey of imagination, determination, and persistence.

Both authors used the same prewriting plan. What is it about the second version that puts it light years ahead of the first?

Have you ever seen the T.V. series *The Wonder Years?* If so, you'll remember the droning voice of the social studies teacher, flatly recounting historical events, reducing their significance with his lack of inflection. The first introduction has that same monotonous, tedious tone, even though it clearly spells out the main ideas for the reader.

The revision, by contrast, touches upon each main idea. The reference to Icarus relates to Main Idea #1 (i.e. ancient desire). The mention of Da Vinci's flying machine relates to Main Idea #2 (i.e. the development of the airplane), and follows a sequential progression to the straightforward statement regarding the space shuttle (i.e. Main Idea #3). Specific examples such as Icarus and Da Vinci bring abstract ideas to life, allowing the reader to wonder. The last sentence clearly and concisely tells the reader what the piece will be all about—the history of flight.

What Do Introduction Paragraphs Need?

Effective introduction paragraphs are made up of two elements: the lead and the thesis statement. The lead is designed to capture the reader's attention. The thesis statement clearly and concisely tells the reader what the piece is all about.

How can students learn to go beyond the boring, point by point "I will tell you about . . ." type of beginning to something that invites readers in, tickles their fancy, and gets them wondering? We begin by analyzing the kinds of introductions that appeal to readers the most.

Some Examples of Introductions That Work

Here is a collection of effective introduction paragraphs which I collected from a variety of magazines. The leads have been circled, the thesis statements underlined.

They're out there. They can be found just off the road, all across America, casting giant shadows. That's because they're giants. They are great big people, animals, and assorted other strange stuff. Most people think they're simply statues, made to advertise a store or a tourist attraction. But we think they may be a bit more interesting, scientifically speaking.

> —from "Monster Watching: A Field Guide to the Really Big Flora and Fauna of America's Roadsides" by Steve Mirsky, *Muse*, July/August 2000

The mirror above the dresser rattles. The lamp begins to flicker. It feels like a giant is gently shaking the room. A few seconds later, the movement stops. The earthquake is over. More than a million earthquakes occur in the world each year.

> —from "When the Earth Moves" by Ann Jordan, *Appleseeds*, February 2001

The pink bubble swells from your lips. Carefully, you puff it full of air. It's big. It's getting bigger. It's the biggest one you've ever made! Suddenly, "POP!" Now you'll have to start over. Your mouth fills with delicious sweetness as you chew. Where does it come from, this wonderful stretchy stuff we call gum? Would you believe it comes from a tree?

> —from "What's That in Your Mouth?" by Carrol J. Swanson, *Boys' Quest*, August/September 1999

> Recently, I was talking to a man whose wife had named their pet goat William E. Goat. They called him lovingly by his nickname, Bill E. Goat. This garbage disposal, cleverly disguised as a goat, is just one of the millions of other pets and animals blessed, or cursed, with not just a name, but a human name.
>
> —from "The Name Game" by Marty Becker, D.V.M., *Pet Life*, July/August 1999

I share these introduction paragraphs with my students by pasting them to a chart and under-lining the leads in red and the thesis statements in blue. I ask the students how they might describe the leads. Many of them notice that the leads are actually Golden Bricks, as described in Chapter 6—that authors use enticing techniques right up front to grab the reader's atten-tion. Students also find bold opinions and series of questions used as leads.

Lesson:

Look at Leads

Here is a lesson I share with my students to help them identify techniques authors use to create leads.

1. I start by talking about the options we've discovered in published pieces: a quote, a statis-tic, an amazing fact, a descriptive segment, bold opinion, and a series of questions, and provide examples of how they could be used effectively in a lead.

2. I put the following information on the overhead and walk students through it:

What Your Introduction Paragraph Needs

A Lead: Catch the reader's attention with:

An amazing or unusual fact	A question
A descriptive segment	A bold opinion
A quote	A statistic

Thesis Statement: Briefly and clearly, tell the reader what the piece will be about.

---

3. We read each of the following introduction paragraphs one by one, paying attention to the different kinds of leads. The leads appear in italics. The thesis statements are underlined and, in all paragraphs, exactly the same, to reinforce that there are many ways to lead the reader into a piece of expository writing.

Type of lead: descriptive segment
Cats: furry and fluffy, sleek and sophisticated, playful and proud. These amazing felines make

the best possible pets!

Type of lead: amazing fact

These celebrities of the animal kingdom have been featured everywhere from Broadway to King Tut's tomb! These amazing felines make the best possible pets!

Type of lead: a bold opinion

They are more intelligent than dogs, cleaner and neater than birds, and less annoying than a sister or a brother. These amazing felines make the best possible pets!

Type of lead: quote

"I'll travel anywhere around the globe to make a picture," says Hollywood superstar Maxine Foster, "as long as I can bring my kitty cat along on the shoot!" These amazing felines make the best possible pets!

Type of lead: statistic

What do more than 20 million Americans have in common? They are the proud owners of the fabulous feline. These amazing felines make the best possible pets!

Type of lead: question

Are you looking for a good companion, a faithful friend, some good clean entertainment? Then look no further. Just buy yourself a cat. These amazing felines make the best possible pets!

There is no doubt that what any of these paragraphs introduces is an expository piece about cats and why they make great pets.

4. I point out that the writer can be as creative as he or she wants to be in constructing an attention-grabbing lead. I also tell students that the writer could have written, "This story will tell you all the reasons that cats make the best pets." But would that have been as inviting?

 # Writing Leads and Thesis Statements

It isn't realistic to expect students to move directly from recognizing various kinds of leads to writing them well. I always provide many opportunities to analyze the techniques before students attempt them.

One way to do this is to present them with a variety of successful introduction paragraphs and ask them to underline the lead in red and the thesis statement in blue. Then, ask them to identify the topic and the kind of lead the author used: quote, statistic, descriptive segment, amazing fact, bold opinion, or question. You might want to use the following examples or others you've found in magazines.

> American philosopher and writer Henry David Thoreau said of the bluebird, "This bird carries the sky on its back." This gentle, beautiful bird is a favorite among bird watchers.
> **Type of lead: quote, TOPIC: bluebirds**

> No refrigerators, no freezers, no canned food. How did the colonists keep their food from spoiling? The answer is sand, sugar, sun, salt, and smoke.
> —from *Appleseeds*, October 2000
> **Type of lead: question/amazing fact, TOPIC: Colonial food preservation**

> Does the thought of creamy milk chocolate make your mouth water? Do crunchy pecans lightly toasted appeal to you? Can't you almost taste the finely grated shreds of scrumptious coconut, resting in a layer of golden caramel? Without a doubt, coco-caramel chocolate candies are wonderful to make, to eat, and to give away!
> **Type of lead: descriptive segment/question, TOPIC: Coco-caramel chocolate candies**

> If I could, I would ban the use of cell phones altogether—collect them up and dump them over a cliff! Good riddance to this most annoying modern techno-logical pest! Cell phones are noisy, intrusive, and hazardous to your health.
> **Type of lead: bold opinion, TOPIC: Cell phones**

> Last year Dave's Dugout served their famous chili-cheeseburgers to over 100,000 delighted customers! His super-deluxe chili-cheeseburger is delicious and eco-nomical too!
> **Type of lead: statistic, TOPIC: Dave's Chili-Cheeseburger**

After reading a number of effective introduction paragraphs, students become adept at identi-fying the topic, type of lead, and the thesis statement.

My colleague Linda Chandler took her class through a revealing follow-up exercise. She dis-tributed a set of expository papers that her students had written prior to learning about leads and thesis statements. Students were asked to reread their papers and draw a circle around their introduction paragraph, a red line under their lead, and a blue line under their thesis statement. The class was astounded to find that most of their introduction paragraphs had weak or missing leads and wishy-washy thesis statements.

Craft Leads

Next, I assist students in revising lackluster leads. I model the following procedure and then make time for guided practice.

1. I begin by displaying a boring introduction paragraph for the class:

> *I like pets—don't you? My report will tell you how pets are fun to play with, the ways they are helpful, and how they become one of the family.*

"Hmmm . . ." I say, "What do you think of this introduction paragraph?"
"Boring!" the students respond.
"What do you think of the lead?" I ask.
A few hands go up.
"Jen?" I ask.
"It's a question, but it's not a very interesting question."
Her classmates agree.

2. "Let's revise this," I say. "Who can help me list all of the possible leads we can use?"

More hands go up this time and suggestions fly. I start the list on the overhead: amazing facts, descriptive segments, bold opinions, questions.

"Why don't we try a descriptive segment?" I ask. "Let's begin by thinking of a few interesting pets."

The students call out a pet store's inventory. "Parakeets, cats, ferrets, gerbils, guinea pigs, tropical fish, lizards, snakes, frogs, dogs, pot-bellied pigs . . ." The list goes on.

"We've got a great variety here. I'm going to describe a little something about a number of these pets." I nibble my lip and begin to write:

> *Finned or fluffy, scaly or slimy, feathered or furry, there are pets that appeal to just about every personality.*

"I like the way each pair of words starts the same," offers Madison.

"Alliteration," I answer, smiling. "Alliteration gives my descriptive segment a little more pizzazz!"

The kids nod.

I go on.

3. I move on to thesis statement. "That's my lead, a descriptive segment. I happened to use alliteration, but it isn't necessary in a descriptive segment. Now, for the thesis statement, what would you say my topic is?"

"Pets," they call out. "How pets are helpful, fun, and part of the family."

"Excellent," I say and add my revised thesis statement to the introduction:

> *Finned or fluffy, scaly or slimy, feathered or furry, there are pets that appeal to just about every personality. A pet is not only fun, but a helpful, important member of the family!*

4. We compare the "before" and "after" versions. Everyone agrees that the "after" version is far better. I also point out that the phrase, "My report will tell you how . . ." in the "before version" is unnecessary. The writer can leave it out and still get the message across, that pets are fun to play with, helpful, and a part of the family, by simply stating, "Pets are . . ." (It's a little like a waitress saying, "This menu will show you that we serve baked stuffed lobster." Why not just say, "We serve baked stuffed lobster"?)

5. We move to guided practice. The students revise the same introduction using their own descriptive segment. I remind them that they don't need to use alliteration, just some vivid words. I walk about as they work, reading examples aloud, discussing what works and what doesn't.

On another day, I repeat that lesson, using a different "before" and "after" paragraph with a different type of lead. After a bit of practice, students begin to write their leads purposefully, with a clear understanding of craft. Their leads dramatically improve.

Writing Thesis Statements That Entice Readers

I remind students that thesis statements should be lucid, clear-cut sentences that tell the reader what they will be reading about. Like a teacher setting a purpose for a lesson, a thesis statement sets an expectation. It encourages the reader to bring prior knowledge to the reading task.

For most young writers in my class, I insist that they include references to each of their main ideas in their thesis statements. In the "real world," authors are less apt to be so strict. Instead, they usually provide an umbrella statement that touches on the content to follow. Compare these two thesis statements on the same topic. One states the main ideas that will follow, the other does not:

Becoming an accomplished musician involves listening, practicing, and performing music. (Main ideas are stated: #1: listening, #2: practicing, #3: performing)

Becoming an accomplished musician involves many things. (This thesis statement does not tell the reader what those skills and practices are, but provides enough information for the reader to focus and to make some predictions.)

Both of these thesis statements work, but I insist that my students practice the first approach because, I've found, it helps them stay focused. It also helps them later when they are restating those main ideas in their conclusions. (More on that topic in the next chapter.) Obviously, though, if a student is writing a research report with many main ideas, stating them in the thesis statement would create a grocery list. So it's important to decide what your expectation will be, given your students' skill levels and the scope of their pieces.

Perhaps the hardest part of writing thesis statements, though, has more to do with structure than content—getting away from that "I will tell you about . . ." beginning that kids seem to favor. I believe that they don't actually favor it, but that they don't have good alternatives at their fingertips. So let's look at options for stating what a piece of writing is all about.

Instead of saying:

I will tell you about the barn owl's appearance, habitat, and diet.

Try any of these "learning about" information statements:

♦ Learning about this nocturnal bird's appearance, habitat, and diet can be an enlightening experience.

♦ Discovering the appearance, habitat, and diet of the barn owl might surprise you.

♦ Naturalists and bird enthusiasts have spent years studying the barn owl, its habitat, and its prey.

♦ Taking the time to become familiar with this bird of prey's appearance, habitat, and diet can be a rewarding experience.

♦ Would you recognize this bird of prey? Could you identify its habitat? Do you know its prey?

♦ You can identify the barn owl by its distinctive appearance. These winged predators can be observed in a variety of habitats, hunting for prey.

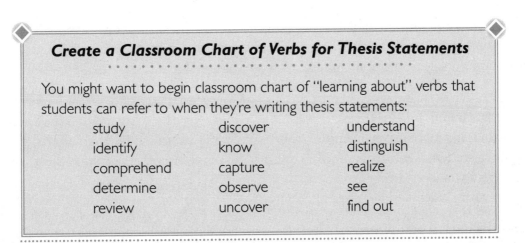

Create a Classroom Chart of Verbs for Thesis Statements

You might want to begin classroom chart of "learning about" verbs that students can refer to when they're writing thesis statements:

study	discover	understand
identify	know	distinguish
comprehend	capture	realize
determine	observe	see
review	uncover	find out

Encourage your students to experiment with sentence starters and informative verbs.

Let's explore . . .	We will uncover . . .
Why not observe . . .	Most people don't realize that . . .
Can you distinguish . . .	It is interesting to study . . .
Let's discover . . .	Do you know that . . .
We can identify . . .	Let's find out about . . .
We can begin to comprehend . . .	Soon you will understand . . .
It has been determined that . . .	Have you ever seen . . .
I will review . . .	It has been shown that . . .

Once you've introduced those sentence starters to your students, try combining them with informative verbs. Once you get started, it will be hard to stop!

Curing the "How Long Should It Be?" Blues

"How long?" or "How many words?" are dreaded questions for a teacher of writing. Determining an effective length of an introduction (or of an entire piece, for that matter) is pretty subjective. This is particularly true for the professional writer who brings a great deal of experience, style, and technique to the craft. A late-breaking newspaper article will probably have a short, bare-bones introduction in order to move the reader quickly to the meat of the piece. The introduction to a gardening article might meander into the body, setting a mood and a tone. Intros to self-help stories in women's magazines often contain column-long anecdotes in order to capture the reader's attention before leading up to a clear thesis statement.

But for most student writers, some kind of expectation is helpful. I usually suggest to my students that they have, minimally, a one sentence lead and one sentence thesis statement: in other words, a two sentence introduction.

For some students, condensing their lead into a single sentence is difficult, especially if they are including a reference to each of their main ideas. So, I suggest a maximum length of five sentences—plenty of room for including main ideas in the basic five-paragraph essay.

I do not encourage students to use anecdotes as leads (although they are often used in published pieces) because it is too easy for them to roll right into a long-winded narrative and mislead the reader about their purpose. And, for so many students, it is difficult to get back on the expository track. The bottom line: I want students to get to the point and devote most of their energy to the body of the piece.

You will find that, regardless of any guideline you provide, you will have at least one student who will write more or less than you suggest, with more than satisfactory results. In that case, if it seems a lucky exception to the "rule," leave it alone. But do try to determine what it is about the writing—the voice, the description, the word choices, the anecdotes—that allows the writer to bend the rules successfully.

From First to Last Impressions

Obviously, first impressions are important. As the holiday season approaches I anticipate plenty of visitors dropping by. My family and I have decided that we cannot possibly usher guests (especially first-timers) through the unfinished laundry room. Instead, we have our guests come to the front door, across the newly restored and painted gingerbread-trimmed porch. It is inviting. As they glance at the long, wavy, century-old glass windows, they raise an eyebrow, eager to enter and see what's inside. And after spending time inside, after forming an overall impression, my guests will leave with some final view of their experience. I hope it's a favorable one. First impressions count, and so do final thoughts.

In the next chapter we'll look at ways students can wrap up a piece of writing so their concluding ideas are as powerfully expressed as those that drew readers in at the beginning.

Chapter 8

Crafting Conclusions

....

Bringing It Full Circle

"Something I often do in my own work is to bring the story full circle—to strike at the end an echo of a note that was sounded at the beginning. It gratifies my sense of symmetry, and it also pleases the reader, completing with its resonance the journeywe set out on together."

—William Zinsser, from *On Writing Well*

William Zinsser's thoughts about symmetry apply to expository writing. The beginning and the ending, the introduction and the conclusion, should balance one another. The ending must, in some way, reiterate what was put forth in the beginning. In fact, that reflects the design of the Expository Pillar, described in Chapter 2, with its broad matching header and footer representing introduction and conclusion.

Read the following introduction and conclusion by a fifth-grade student:

> Introduction:
> *What is as fast as an automobile, as spotty as a Dalmatian, and prowls jungles and grasslands for prey? The cheetah, that's what! You will learn how fast cheetahs run, what they look like, and where these interesting felines live.*

> Conclusion:
> *So, now you know how fast cheetahs run, what they look like, and where these interesting felines live. THE END*

This conclusion mirrors the thesis statement in the introduction, and each main idea (e.g. speed, appearance, habitat) is reiterated. But is it a successful, effective conclusion? Does it leave the reader with a lasting impression? Not really. This conclusion is redundant, dull, and abrupt, in my opinion.

Unfortunately, it is also typical of most conclusion paragraphs in the student work I see. Children often have great difficulty restating their main ideas effectively. How can we help them craft conclusions that serve to reiterate their main ideas in interesting, creative ways?

Types of Conclusions and How to Teach Them

A Series of Questions

One of the easiest ways to avoid the boring conclusion is to reiterate each main idea as a question. In the cheetah piece, the main ideas deal with speed, appearance, and habitat. Therefore, a better conclusion might be:

> *So, can you name the speediest of all the big cats? Can you describe this handsome creature? Were you surprised to learn where these interesting felines live?*

While the revision helps, the conclusion is still abrupt. It is crying out for a final sentence, something broader than a regurgitation of main ideas. I sometimes ask students for a few words that sum up their impression of their topic. In this case, I might ask, "Give me one or two adjectives that best describe the cheetah." Responses might include: beautiful, amazing, interesting, fascinating, remarkable, exciting. Adding an opinion to the end, a gut reaction, lends a feeling of finality—the proverbial last word.

> *So, can you name the speediest of all the big cats? Can you describe this handsome creature? Were you surprised to learn where these interesting felines live? The cheetah is a remarkable member of the animal kingdom.*

That final sentence is a good example of the nonspecific thesis statement, because the individual main ideas are not referenced. While statements like these in the introduction might prevent a student from focusing, they can do no harm in the conclusion. In fact, they can function perfectly.

Also notice that in this revised version "The End" was eliminated, since the writer did not need to state the obvious. (Although, for many of us, writing the words "The End" provides a real sense of accomplishment!)

This technique, of asking questions and capping them off with an umbrella statement, can work with just about any topic. Look at this prewriting plan, for example.

TOPIC: Lemonade
Main Idea #1 - Easy to Make
Main Idea #2 - Delicious and Refreshing
Main Idea #3 - Set up a Lemonade Stand

Here's how this student used a series of questions to reference each main idea in the conclusion of her piece:

> *So, what could be more convenient than tearing open that handy packet of lemonade mix, adding water, and stirring? Can you think of anything more tangy and refreshing? And, have you ever considered selling your surplus lemonade at a stand on a bustling street corner? These are just three reasons that lemonade is the best drink around!*

Adding a vivid adjective (convenient, handy, tangy, surplus, bustling) to each restated main idea gives the overall conclusion sparkle.

Word Referents and Adjectives

Another cure for unmemorable conclusions is to use word referents and adjectives, as described in Chapter 4. For example, I might ask the writer of the original cheetah conclusion, on page 106, to brainstorm a number of word referents to replace redundant key words or phrases:

Cheetah: fast cat, feline speed machine, spotted sprinters, big, sleek cats
What they look like: appearance, good looks, attractive characteristics

Where they live: habitat, domain, range, territory

Even if the too-chatty sentence starter "So, now you know . . ." doesn't change, using word referents in place of key words or phrases, as well as the umbrella statement at the end, can improve the conclusion. Here's a revision of the cheetah conclusion with word referents substituted for key words or phrases:

> *So, now you know how fast these feline speed machines run, you can recognize them by their attractive characteristics, and become familiar with their habitat and range. The cheetah is a remarkable member of the animal kingdom.*

The use of a variety of informative verbs (know, recognize, become familiar with) also adds variety to the conclusion.

The first sentence is the only part that still cries out for attention. "So, now you know . . ." has a humdrum, pedestrian tone. (It is a little like its counterpart "I will tell you about . . ." that appears in so many introductions.) But you can't tell students, "You see this phrase? It's a little boring, please don't use it," unless you want to deflate them entirely. If you take away a comfortable convention, you must help students find a practical alternative.

The Hypothetical Anecdote

The hypothetical anecdote is a device authors use all the time to lead the reader smoothly into the conclusion. It involves relating the topic to some hypothetical experience that the reader might have had. Here's an example:

> *If you should ever have the good fortune to go on safari, be on the lookout for the cheetah. Perhaps you'll get to see first hand how fast these feline speed machines run, you'll be able to recognize their attractive characteristics, and become better acquainted with their habitat and range. The cheetah is a remarkable member of the animal kingdom.*

I generated this hypothetical anecdote by asking myself where I might see a cheetah. Another example:

> *The next time you visit the zoo make sure to see the magnificent cheetah. Perhaps you'll get to see first hand how fast these feline speed machines run, you'll be able to recognize their attractive characteristics, and you'll become better acquainted with their habitat and range. The cheetah is a remarkable member of the animal kingdom.*

Creating a hypothetical anecdote is fairly easy. After you've shown students some examples, provide them with a list of topics and, together, come up with a hypothetical anecdote for each. (See the chart below.) I ask students these questions to get them thinking:

♦ Where might you come in contact with your topic?

♦ Where might you go to learn more about it?

♦ What kinds of activities might allow you to get to know your topic even better?

This chart lists sample topics, "where" and "what" questions to ask, and a sample hypothetical anecdote:

Topic	Where/What Activity	Hypothetical Anecdote
Spiders	attic, basement, garden	Next time you're cleaning out your attic, basement, or garden, be on the lookout for the amazing spider.
Helicopter	taking a trip	If taking a car trip on the expressway stresses you out, consider taking a helicopter instead.
The radio	car, beach	So, whether riding along the open highway in your car or sunning yourself on a sandy beach, be sure to tune in your informative, entertaining radio.
Abe Lincoln	Washington D.C., library	If you ever have the opportunity to visit Washington D.C., visit the Lincoln Memorial.
Poodle	pet shop, dog show	By now you're probably ready to set off to the nearest pet store and buy yourself a standard poodle.
Making friends	school, sports, hobbies	Whether you're involved in team sports, music or dance, or you just enjoy socializing at school, you'll find new friends just about everywhere!

A hypothetical anecdote gives the author a context for referencing each main idea. And it gives the reader an invitation to learn more about the topic through personal experience. This lends a personal touch to the end of a piece.

The Straightforward Conclusion

There are times when a hypothetical anecdote is inappropriate. For example, if the assignment is for students to demonstrate everything they know about the Revolutionary War and the intended audience is the teacher, then they do not need to generate personal interest at the end through the hypothetical anecdote. In fact, the hypothetical anecdote might serve as a distraction. In this kind of piece, or a straightforward research paper, it is more acceptable to stick to the facts and to reiterate the main ideas in the conclusion in a straightforward manner. Compare the next two conclusion paragraphs, each written in response to an essay test question on the Revolutionary War.

Hypothetical Anecdote:
If you are a history buff, I'm sure you enjoyed hearing all about the Revolutionary War. The causes leading up to war with the English, the major battles, and the Colonists' victory must be particularly exciting to read about. It was a war that changed the course of history!

The conversational tone tends to minimize the seriousness of this topic. And, asking your history teacher if he or she is a history buff is probably not a good idea. For the purpose of an exam essay or research report, the following conclusion would be more suitable:

Straightforward Conclusion:
As you can see, the complex causes leading up to the Revolutionary War, the major battles, and the Colonists' victory made a strong impression on the American way of life. It was a war that changed the course of history!

The lead-in to this conclusion ("As you can see . . .") is a solid, no-nonsense approach to this kind of conclusion. Other straightforward lead-ins include "It is clear that . . ." "Without a doubt . . ." and "Certainly . . ."

Notice the way these can be used almost interchangeably in this conclusion:

Certainly, the complex causes leading up to the Revolutionary War, the major battles, and the Colonists' victory made a strong impression on the American way of life. It was a war that changed the course of history!

It is clear that the complex causes leading up to the Revolutionary War, the major battles, and the Colonists' victory made a strong impression on the American way of life. It was a war that changed the course of history!

Without a doubt, the complex causes leading up to the Revolutionary War, the major battles, and the Colonists' victory made a strong impression on the American way of life. It was a war that changed the course of history!

Unquestionably, the complex causes leading up to the Revolutionary War, the major battles, and the Colonists' victory made a strong impression on the American way of life. It was a war that changed the course of history!

Clearly, the complex causes leading up to the Revolutionary War, the major battles, and the Colonists' victory made a strong impression on the American way of life. It was a war that changed the course of history!

The Last Word on Conclusions

When all is said and done, the conclusion paragraph should sum up the piece of writing, reiterate the main ideas with style, and drive home, with a broad umbrella statement, the main thrust of the piece. In short, the conclusion should review and reinforce what has been fully elaborated earlier on. In fact, I tell my students that based on their conclusion alone, the reader should be able to reconstruct the simple prewriting plan on which the piece was built, including the topic and main ideas.

Most important, a well-crafted conclusion ensures that the reader walks away with a strong impression. As the saying goes, "all's well that ends well."

Create a Chart of Lead-Ins

You might want to maintain a classroom chart of lead-ins that students can refer to when they're writing straightforward conclusions:

As you can see
It is clear that
Certainly
Clearly
Without a doubt
Most would agree that
Indeed
Surely
Unquestionably
Obviously

Chapter 9

Establishing
Voice, Tone, and Slant

At a recent workshop on expository writing a teacher approached me and said, "You use first person quite a lot in the modeling you do. You don't seem concerned with using 'I' or 'you.' I was always taught that this kind of first-person, conversational tone is not appropriate in expository writing."

I knew where she was coming from. The examples we constructed during the workshop were often light, spirited, and generously peppered with first-person pronouns. In contrast, when I was in school, terms such as expository text, research paper, report, and essay conjured up images of weighty, dry textbooks with small print, footnotes, bibliographies, and that encyclopedic voice that forces you to read the same paragraph over and over again.

But, fortunately, text that delivers information effectively doesn't have to be, well, boring. Expository writing can and should be lively as well as informative. How many times have you been captivated by a well-written magazine piece or newspaper article or stood around a bookstore for an hour immersed in a nonfiction book on gardening, child care, or home improvement?

Using first person in exposition is not simply a stylistic preference of mine. In *On Writing Well: The Classic Guide to Writing Nonfiction*, William Zinsser discusses its use:

"What I'm always looking for as an editor is a sentence that says something like 'I'll never forget the day when I . . .' I think, Aha! A person!

"Writers are obviously at their most natural when they write in the first person. Writing is an intimate transaction between two people, conducted on paper, and it will go well to the extent that it retains its humanity. Therefore I urge people to write in the first person: to use 'I' and 'me" and 'we' and 'us'."

What Zinsser is talking about here is not only the use of first person, but also voice, tone, and slant.

> **Voice:** The reader's impression of who is "speaking" through the writing. The word choice, phrasing, and style reflect the point of view, attitudes, and personality of the writer.
>
> **Tone:** The mood or atmosphere a writer sets through word choice and literary style. For example, an essay that criticizes an administration's ecological policies might use words like "problem," "headache," and "dire situation." An essay presenting a more positive view of the same policies might use words like "challenge," "question," and "circumstance" to describe the same events. The difference is in the connotation.
>
> **Slant:** The angle that a writer adopts in aiming a piece at a particular audience. An author will slant the piece differently depending on who is likely to be reading it. Authors usually determine the slant first, then adjust the voice and the tone accordingly.

Many times, I've found myself absorbed in nonfiction articles on topics that initially were of little interest to me, simply because the information was presented in an appealing way. The author really "sold" me on the topic through an interesting slant, authentic voice, and compelling tone.

The Velcro Piece

One memorable article was on Velcro, of all things. (I can't remember the source, but the facts have certainly stuck with me, no pun intended.) Because of an intriguing introduction and a number of amazing facts, I devoured the article, start to finish. I also got the feeling that the author was speaking to me, not at me.

Read these two paragraphs based on what I learned about Velcro and decide which is more effective. Which one uses slant, voice, and tone to reach the reader?

1. The material commonly known as Velcro is thought to be important in many ways. Like many inventions, the development of Velcro was based on an observation from nature. After observing the way that the small hook-like petals on the plant commonly referred to as the nettle stuck to fibrous surfaces, scientists recreated strips of heavy duty hook and loop-like fabric that adhere together in similar fashion. Velcro has proven to be extremely helpful to society in many ways. Medical professionals use it in surgical settings. It can be used inside military tanks to hold equipment in place. It is reported that NASA places Velcro on the inside of space helmets in order for astronauts to have a rough surface against which they can rub their faces, which are said to be prone to dryness and irritation during space travel. Additionally, one can find Velcro in use in many ways in most modern American households.

2. It seems to me that Velcro is the most amazingly simple, yet incredibly versatile invention known to modern man (and woman!). Based on the principles of the annoying wild weed known as the nettle, Velcro is comprised of a series of tiny hooks and loops. A strip of Velcro sticks to its companion piece with as much stubborn determination as a nettle sticks to the fiber of your brand new cashmere sweater! Because of its ability to hang onto things, Velcro is the perfect solution for many sticky situations you might find yourself in. Velcro is used in everything from open heart surgery, keeping small body parts in place during tricky medical procedures, to the insides of army tanks, where it is used to hold tools to the walls in handy, easy to reach locations. I was really tickled to learn that Velcro is even placed on the inside of NASA astronauts' space helmets. Why, you ask? So that these high tech space travelers have a rough surface on which to scratch an itchy nose or cheek! You don't have to have surgery, join the *army, or become an astronaut to benefit from Velcro. The next time you'd like to secure those running shoes that you're too lazy to lace, or when you need to mount your portable cup holder to the console in your aging vehicle, don't fret—just think Velcro!*

While the first paragraph is well written and thorough, there is an impersonal feeling about it. Phrases like, "Velcro is thought to be . . ." ". . . has proven to be . . ." "It is reported that . . ." and "One can find . . ." are wordy and cold. When I read, "It is reported that . . ." I wonder, "Who reported it?" When I read, "One can find . . ." I think, "Who can find?" Zinsser is right. Where is the person, the humanity, in the writing? Who can the reader relate to?

I'm not sure that I would persevere and read an entire article on a subject like Velcro if it were written in the style of the first example. While the facts are interesting, there is nothing of the author in it. The author has no voice.

◀ Activity: ▶

Explore One Topic in Two Voices

An interesting and fun activity that demonstrates this point involves locating magazine articles on a number of topics. Then, look up the same topics in the encyclopedia. Examine the writing side by side, magazine article paired with the corresponding encyclopedia entry. Which is more reader-friendly? This is not to say that encyclopedias are poorly written. But, contributors to magazines and authors of nonfiction books are given the time and space to address audience, style, and tone. Encyclopedia writers need to include as much information on a broad range of topics in as little space as possible. Slant, tone, and voice fall by the wayside in the process.

My Slant on Slant

Even when providing straight information, authors naturally slant their writing in some way. In other words, they keep their own attitudes, opinions, or point of view in there to some degree. This does not mean that every piece of expository writing is persuasive. However, a writer with an authentic voice is not afraid to present information in a way that feels personally credible, responsible, and true.

For example, imagine an article titled: "Our Shrinking Woodlands". The balance and weight the author gives pieces of information determine the article's slant. Is the author beginning with the personal view that our forests are doomed to development and pollution? If so, the author will probably place more emphasis on facts that support this view. On the other hand, if the author embraces the idea that moving toward designated sanctuaries, land trusts, and open spaces is a positive, hopeful sign, the piece will be weighted that way.

Whichever the author's message, the language and tone need to be consistent throughout the piece, so as not to confuse or mislead the reader. This is not to say that a writer cannot present two sides or views of an issue. In fact, an evenly balanced piece will present both sides, but the way in which this information is developed depends on the slant.

Audience Impact on Voice, Tone, and Slant

Of course, the writer must determine the audience before beginning. An expository piece on flight intended for NASA scientists would differ in content, vocabulary, and tone from an expository piece on flight for the average commercial airline passenger. If you want your readers to read, understand, and enjoy the piece, knowing your audience is critical.

Read these two paragraphs, both written on the same topic (school cafeteria meals) but for different audiences. The first was slanted to address parents' concerns, the second toward children's.

1. Our brand new school cafeteria provides many healthy food choices for your child. Each daily menu is designed to include the correct balance of each of the food groups based on the Health Department's food pyramid. Since we are aware that most children will not eat food that does not appeal to them, we also take into account children's culinary tastes, likes, and dislikes. Tasty, low-fat versions of favorite foods such as pizza, hot dogs, burgers, and chicken nuggets have been developed. You can be assured that our cafeteria staff works very hard to ensure that your child receives healthy, delicious meals here at school.

2. If you ask most kids what their favorite part of the day is, they'll say lunch! After all, what's not to like in our new and improved school cafeteria? Think you need to head to the local fast food place for juicy burgers and tasty chicken nuggets? Now, you can enjoy these awesome foods right in your very own school! And let's not forget hot dogs and pizza, all prepared without the grease that can turn a perfectly good meal into a high fat oil slick on your lunch tray! Service with a smile and delicious, attractive foods that are low fat to boot. Is it any wonder lunch might just become your favorite part of the day?

Both paragraphs stress that the new cafeteria provides food that is appealing to children and is, at the same time, healthy and low in fat. However, the writer was aware of the preferences of the two audiences. The first paragraph takes into account parents' concern that kids get a balanced, healthy lunch. The second paragraph is designed to appeal to kids' taste buds and sense of humor. Since parents' concerns are more "serious," the tone of the first piece is more serious. The writer is aware that children often resist what's good for them and, therefore, in the second piece, focuses on flavor and keeps the tone light. Keeping your audience in mind as you write is critical. Imagine sending paragraph one to students, and paragraph two to parents!

You can present these ideas to your students by reading aloud both paragraphs without any introduction and seeing if they can identify the intended audience of each.

Unity of Voice, Tone, and Slant

Recently I came home from a workshop, entered my lovely new kitchen, and stopped short. Sitting on the counter, beside a small collection of antique baskets, was a sleek, asymmetrical chrome bowl full of fruit. It was very attractive. But it didn't belong in my Victorian kitchen. My husband walked in, pleased as could be, explaining how he'd received it as a gift, and asking me how I liked it. Well, I told him I liked it just fine, and since it was a gift to him he ought to display it in his office. It just didn't fit. In fact, it stuck out like a sore thumb.

Writing also needs unity throughout in order to work. A unified piece of writing never misleads the reader or distracts him or her by changing in voice, tone, and slant. For example, what do you think of this paragraph about the new school cafeteria?

> Our brand new school cafeteria provides many healthy food choices for your child. Each daily menu is designed to include the correct balance of each of the food groups based on the Health Department's food pyramid. Since we are aware that most children will not eat food that does not appeal to them, we also take into account children's culinary tastes, likes, and dislikes. Think your child needs to head to the local fast food place for juicy burgers and tasty chicken nuggets? Now, they can enjoy these awesome foods right in our very own school! And let's not forget hot dogs and pizza, all prepared without the grease that can turn a perfectly good meal into a high fat oil slick on your lunch tray! You can be assured that our cafeteria staff works very hard to ensure that your child receives healthy, delicious meals here at school.

Were you thrown a little when you got to the fourth and fifth sentences? Was it as though another author picked up and continued on, until sentence six, where the first voice resurfaces? The writer needs to decide up front what kind of tone to take on an expository piece and stick with it. She might choose a journalistic report tone, a polite or formal conversational tone, or a familiar, humorous tone. Will the piece be slanted toward an emphasis on nutrition or on the culinary preferences of the average child? Whatever she decides, it is important to remain consistent throughout the piece.

I will sometimes ask students who they want to be as they assume the role of information provider/author in the piece they are writing. Here are some questions that help students define their voice. I'm careful to remind them that a sensitivity to audience affects the voice, tone, and slant they take.

Do you see yourself as an expert on your subject? If so, you'll want your audience to take you quite seriously, and your tone should be that of a news reporter, a professor, a scientist, or a historian.

Do you see yourself sharing information you've learned with a new neighbor or an acquaintance? If so, your tone should be personal but polite and formal.

Do you see yourself sharing information with an audience of people mostly like you—people you know and understand well? If so, your tone should be casual. Your writing should read the way you speak every day, so don't be afraid to inject humor and personal opinion. Your audience will not only learn about your topic but about you as a person.

In effective expository writing, audience, slant, tone, and voice are critically linked. When you "speak" honestly to your audience, your writing feels authentic. So students need to decide to whom they are writing and express themselves as they would speak to that audience.

Teaching Voice, Slant, Tone

Voice, slant, and tone are sophisticated, often subjective aspects of writing and cannot be taught as much as they can be discussed and recognized. The best way to raise students' awareness of voice, slant, and tone is to read and discuss many, many articles and compare them. For example, read aloud a terrific article in Smithsonian's *Muse* on an unusual topic and compare it to an encyclopedia entry on the same topic. (I recently chose zippers as a topic!)

After reading, ask students what they surmise about the author's feelings on the subject. Can they make some assumptions about the author's personality? Is he or she bubbly and positive, cynical, suspicious, adventurous, worn out, angry, an eternal optimist, fair-minded, logical and deliberate, opinionated, humorous, or fun-loving? What hints does the author provide that lead us to make those assumptions? The fact is, the stronger the voice, tone, and slant, the more accurate those assumptions can be.

Voice, slant, and tone emerge when the writer moves beyond mechanics and begins to speak honestly and authentically to his or her audience. As teachers of writing, we must help children master all the skills necessary for effective writing, writing attention-grabbing introductions, generating broad, yet distinct, main idea sentences, creating powerful supporting details, crafting effective conclusions, and using vivid words and good sentence structure and variety, so that mechanics become second nature. Then voice, slant, and tone begin to emerge on their own.

Chapter 10

Putting It All Together

Weaving Strategies into Writers' Workshop

At the beginning of this book, I talked about how I struggled to manage writers' workshop. Then, for nine chapters, I have talked about how I teach the skills students need to write effective expository pieces and how I provide opportunities for them to practice those skills in isolation. But what about applying those skills in the context of real writing? Students must have opportunities to craft their pieces over time, putting them aside for a day or two, thinking, rehashing, revising, and editing, before publishing. That is, after all, what writers do in the real world.

Knowing that students need process writing time and knowing that I was not great at managing conferences, I began to reevaluate the way I implemented process writing.

The Process-Writing Timeline

The procedure I developed, which I call the Process-Writing Timeline, is guided and directed. It provides a context for all the strategies I've discussed thus far. Rather than restraining creativity, it gives students a more structured, comfortable framework within which to write. It also moves the process along to help students progress in a more timely way without being mired in a piece for weeks. In fact, we were able to complete more pieces, with a greater level of success, without sacrificing peer sharing and conversation. Here's the timeline I follow; yours may be different, depending on your goals and your students' needs. Keep in mind that these days need not be consecutive.

Day 1, Prewriting Plan: I assign a broad theme related to our curriculum, such as the "woodland habitat," which ensures that students have a good knowledge base from which to work. I ask students to choose a topic relating to the theme, perhaps a woodland animal or issue such as forest fires. I model the Pick, List, and Choose procedure as explained in Chapter 3. and have the whole class help me create a basic prewriting plan. For example, my topic might be "deer" and, using Pick, List, and Choose, I might come up with the following plan:

> TOPIC: Deer
> Main Idea #1: Appearance
> Main Idea #2: Diet
> Main Idea #3: Behavior

Students use the same procedure to think through their own topics. By the end of our session, they each have a prewriting plan. I collect the plans and look them over, checking for main ideas that are too broad or too narrow. We discuss these as a class on Day 2.

Day 2, Introduction Paragraph: I share a number of prewriting plans with the entire class. Then we discuss the introduction paragraph. If we haven't worked on introduction paragraphs yet, I keep the conversation simple: "The introduction must tell the reader what the entire piece will be about. Be sure to include each main idea." If we have studied introduction paragraphs, I review the various kinds of leads and ask students to choose one. As they work, I walk around, checking everyone's progress. Because we're only working on the introduction, I can usually have a short conference with everyone. I share terrific examples. For students who finish their introductions early, I have a related art, mapping, or graphing project, which prevents them from zooming ahead carelessly and "finishing" the piece. I meet with students who might be struggling while others work on their projects.

Day 3, Main Idea Sentences: I review how to translate main-idea blurbs into well-structured main-idea sentences, as explained in Chapter 4. I talk about synonymous words and phrases students might use in place of their blurbs. Students brainstorm some phrases and write them on index cards. I point to our class chart containing all the ways to begin main-idea sentences. Then students write a main-idea sentence for each blurb. I circulate as they work, pointing out vivid examples to the whole class. Again, as they finish, they move to a related project.

Day 4, Supporting Details: I review the detail-generating questions as explained in Chapter 5, and, if we've covered it, Golden Bricks explained in Chapter 6. Then I encourage students to write supporting details for their first main-idea sentence. I circulate, looking for good sentence variety, colorful descriptions, and so forth. I never have students take on more than a single paragraph a day, so that I can touch base with all of them and share thoughts before they move ahead. Therefore, on Days 5 and 6 students work on different paragraphs, revising and elaborating as they go. Sometimes I take paragraphs home and write specific comments to guide revision.

Day 7, Conclusion Paragraph: I review the conclusion paragraph and have students write their own, as explained in Chapter 8. Again, I circulate as they work, and we discuss various examples.

Day 8, Final Check: Students revise and edit. Since I've been checking their work all along, and they've been revising and editing all along, this step is generally not that complicated. Usually they are ready to publish their work.

With the Process-Writing Timeline, students not only apply each skill they've learned, but they move along in a timely, productive way. Because of the single theme, they can relate to the work of others and use what they learn in their own work. The best part, though, is that in eight sessions everyone's completed an expository piece. No one is bored. In fact, students are delighted with the polished work they've created, along with projects they've completed to accompany their writing.

The Importance of Student Accountability

Over the years, I've had an occasional student who will dig in his or her heels and resist any suggestions for revision. I always struggled with this, because I didn't want to dictate or override the student's sense of ownership. Yet, at times, I felt as though the student was simply avoiding the difficult process of revision. I never knew how hard to push and often felt as if I, along with the student, was copping out.

I've come up with a reasonable way to handle that situation, keeping two objectives in mind: to always respect the student's voice and intent, and to ensure that he or she has mastered the important strategies I've taught. So, when a student resists revision, I insist on evidence that he or she can do what I'm asking. For example, if a student has stated only facts in a piece, and is resisting my suggestion to apply detail-generating questions, I might respond this way: "Since you are the author here, you do own the work. While I feel strongly that revision would help, it is your choice whether to do it for your final piece. However, as your teacher, I must have proof that you've mastered this skill. So, what I need you to do is to complete this revision in your journal. That way we will both be satisfied."

This approach is reasonable. And I practice it in all other subject areas as well. Imagine a student doing a less than effective job on long division, and when you point it out, the student replies, "I like it the way it is." Would you ever consider not holding the student accountable? I feel strongly that students must be held equally accountable in writing, and we do them a disservice by not insisting that they work to master essential skills.

State Assessments—Helping Students Do Their Best

In many states, timed writing assessments are a way of life. Students are presented with a prompt and are expected to respond independently in writing, usually within a 45 minute time period. The idea is for them to demonstrate the skills they've mastered.

Of course, it is difficult for students to apply everything they've learned in so little time. In fact, trying to apply all the skills often impedes their ability to concentrate on their writing and the results often don't reflect what they are capable of doing.

Therefore, in order for students to be successful at timed assessments, we need to teach them how to analyze prompts quickly and pace themselves as they plan and write. That way, the assessment tool does not become a roadblock to demonstrating good writing skills.

Preparing Students for Writing Prompts

Lesson:

Plan Your Responses

I make a point to analyze a number of prompts with my students, so they understand how to plan their response. Here is a typical lesson.

1. I show the students an expository prompt that might be on the test:

If you could have any pet, what kind of pet would you choose? Write about this pet and about what it would be like to own and care for it.

2. First I ask, what are the givens? In other words, what does everyone have to write about? A pet. Next I ask, what are the variables? In other words, what does the author need to decide? The kind of pet he or she would choose and the care it requires.

3. I have students brainstorm a simple prewriting plan:

TOPIC: Guinea Pig
Main Idea #1: Appearance
Main Idea #2: Supplies You Need
Main Idea #3: Behavior

4. Since my objective at this stage is to show how to approach prompts in an efficient way, I don't encourage students to take this piece further. Instead, I stress that the purpose of timed writing assessments is to show off what they know about writing; their topic is the vehicle for showing that. They do not need to spend a tremendous amount of time determining, for example, which is really their favorite pet. I advise students to pick what they know a lot about and get started quickly. Do not get hung up on phrases like "your favorite" or "the best." Simply choose something you can talk about and go.

Lesson:

Pace Yourself

Keeping track of time and using it wisely can be difficult for many students. Knowing how to pace themselves is critical. So, prior to the test date, it's important to walk them through the process, section by section. I use the following guide for the standard 45 minute testing block:

Plan (read the prompt, write your simple prewriting plan): 5 minutes
Draft introduction paragraph: 5 minutes
Draft the body of the piece (at least 3 paragraphs): 25 minutes
Draft the conclusion: 5 minutes
Reread and edit: 5 minutes

Practice runs are important so that, during the actual test, students are familiar with the planning and pacing necessary to be successful.

1. I give students a prompt, such as:

> Most people like to travel. Write about a place you've been to or a place you'd like to go. Explain what the place has to offer as a vacation destination.

2. We spend exactly five minutes determining the givens and variables and constructing the prewriting plan:

> Givens: Everyone writes about a particular place
> Variables: The particular destination and its appealing characteristics

> TOPIC: Disney World
> Main Idea #1: Great Resorts
> Main Idea #2: Rides
> Main Idea #3: Shows and Parades

3. I briefly review introductions and give students exactly five minutes to write their own. I watch for the students who have trouble finishing and plan to give them additional practice on introductions.

4. We move on to the body of the piece, usually three paragraphs. Students write each paragraph, pausing in between for direction and encouragement. I give them pacing suggestions periodically such as, "You should probably be finishing paragraph one of the body of your piece" and "Let's get into your next main idea." If they fall behind in one paragraph, I encourage them to pick up the pace a little in the next.

Timed writing assessments should not be administered too close together. I visited a district recently where they happened once a week. Now, I ask you, how much growth can occur in seven days? What began as an assessment became a drill, and it no longer served its purpose of demonstrating children's growth over time. Ideally, prompts should be administered once every other month, and certainly not more than once a month.

Scoring Writing Prompts

In my district, prompts are generally evaluated by two readers and assigned a holistic score, based on a rubric. The rubric I use is on the next page. I also share this rubric with my students for self-assessment.

Expository Writing Rubric

0 Unscorable! Wrote nothing or did not write to the prompt.

1 Lots of Room for Improvement! Way too short. No evidence of an organizational plan. No details. Hard to read and understand.

2 Still Has a Way to Go! There may be some paragraphing but main-idea sentences may be missing or unsupported. Don't let the indents fool you—this piece has little if any organization. Details are general (for example, "nice," "cool," "fun"). Weak sentence variety and word choice. Usually missing an introduction and/or conclusion.

3 Almost There! Has an introduction. The lead is weak and the thesis statement a bit unclear. Some evidence of organization and at least three paragraphs in the body. Main-idea sentences may be broad and overlapping or too narrow. Details are mostly general. Few adjectives and interesting words. Has a conclusion in which the main ideas are redundantly restated.

4 Good! Has a satisfactory organizational plan: an adequate introduction with a lead and a thesis statement, at least three paragraphs in the body, and an adequate conclusion that restates the main ideas. Each paragraph has a broad, yet distinct, main idea. Has a mix of general and specific details. Uses at least some interesting words. Main ideas restated in conclusion.

5 Great! Has a strong organizational plan: an effective introduction with a catchy lead, a clear, concise thesis statement, and at least three paragraphs in the body, each with a broad, yet distinct, main-idea sentence. Each main idea is supported by at least four mostly specific details including descriptive segments, anecdotes, and quotes. Mostly uses good sentence variety and word choice. There is a conclusion in which the main ideas are restated.

6 Fantastic! Wow! Has strong organization; a terrific lead; clear thesis statement; at least three body paragraphs, each with a broad, yet distinct, main idea and plenty of specific, powerful supporting details including descriptive segments, anecdotes, statistics, and amazing facts. Excellent word choice and sentence variety make it smooth and interesting to read. Conclusion creatively restates the main ideas.

A score point 4 (or a combined score of 8 if two readers each assigned the piece a 4), would meet my state, Connecticut's, goal for writing profiency. Of course, most students will not meet this goal immediately. As they continue to learn key skills and apply them, the scores will increase.

Another reason for not administering prompts too frequently: A student could show respectable growth over a month, but simply move from a "low 3" to a "high 3" a month later. Of course, telling the student that he or she once again scored below the goal can be discouraging and misleading if there was clear evidence of growth. It's better to leave the score off the student's paper and keep it for your instructional purposes only. Students benefit much more from concrete praise and constructive criticism.

Conclusion

By definition, my conclusion should sum up my main ideas and restate them creatively. But it should also tell a little more, in a way that reveals the heart of the entire work, which is what I will attempt.

Writing is a complex process. It is strengthened by reading with an awareness of the author's purpose, audience, and voice and by allowing reading to become a revealing prewriting experience. Writers develop, as all artists do, by practicing important skills and applying them in personal ways.

Becoming a writer is a journey—a journey that is made smoother through solid instruction and clear expectations. When the instruction is solid, when the writer/traveler has had a wide range of experiences, he or she can tackle whatever obstacles present themselves and begin to enjoy the journey. And, most assuredly, as students, and later as adults in the workforce, there will be many writing obstacles to face.

I recently read an article in *The New York Times* about a consulting firm that charges corporations over 5,000 dollars a day to train employees (most of whom are entry-level college grads) how to write well. I imagine young adults such as my daughter and her peers, those who balked at the college essay and who continue to struggle with expository writing in college and beyond, as being the beneficiaries of the service this company provides. But how much more would they have benefited from good instruction in expository writing beginning in elementary school? I'd wager that if students began their journey as serious writers sooner, that consulting firm would have a much smaller market down the line. And those young employees would have the benefit of years of experience as confident, effective writers.

Eventually, the journey to becoming a writer becomes more than the sum of its parts. It becomes a powerful means of self-discovery and self-expression. What better means do we have to explore, organize, and communicate our ideas, observations, and information to others? What better way for others to reflect on what we say? Writing helps the author and the reader define the world and his or her place in it.

You can truly empower your students in their quest to become fluent, capable writers. My hope is that you use the ideas in this book not only to teach better but also to enrich your own journey. Bon voyage!

Notes